Do You Mind
If I Smoke?

FENELLA FIELDING

Do You Mind If I Smoke?

Fenella Fielding and Simon McKay

PETER OWEN PUBLISHERS

PETER OWEN PUBLISHERS
Conway Hall, 25 Red Lion Square,
London WC1R 4RL, UK

Peter Owen books are distributed in the USA and Canada
by Independent Publishers Group/Trafalgar Square,
814 North Franklin Street, Chicago, IL 60610, USA

First published in Great Britain 2017 by Peter Owen Publishers
Reprinted 2017

© 2017

ISBN 978-0-7206-1991-1

A catalogue record for this book is available from the British Library.

Cover and book design: Etienne Gilfillan
Cover image: StudioCanal
Title page illustration: Jonathan Edwards

Printed by Printfinder, Riga, Latvia

Contents

Foreword

I met Fenella in a west London Pilates class in March 2011. I
didn't know she was famous when she dropped her mat next
to mine, but I liked the look of her and I wondered what her
story was. We spoke a few times before it occurred to me that I
knew her from *Carry On Screaming*, but I honestly didn't think
she looked old enough to have been in a film made in 1966.
(I had no idea what else she'd done. My expertise is in post-
punk and soul music.)

One Saturday morning the Pilates teacher didn't turn
up. We were waiting together; we were chatting. The teacher
really wasn't coming so we went for coffee. Coffee became a
regular thing and I quickly recognised the blindingly obvious:
Fenella is an incredible raconteur. I loved her stories and I
knew we had to do something with them. She was resistant
at first. We kept talking. I upped the ante by buying cakes to
go with the coffee. I think she succumbed, finally, when I said,
'How about ice cream?' I think that was our big moment of
mutual understanding.

In July 2011 we began a long series of meetings every
Thursday at the now defunct Café Rouge on Chiswick High
Road. Very kindly, the manager let us sit in the basement,
which had tables that were rarely used. Each week I'd

come back with new questions. I'd let Fenella talk and I'd say as little as possible; just let her go. I recorded and later transcribed every word. I discovered she had appointment diaries that went back to childhood. There are a few gaps in the years, but in the appendix of this book there's a straight run of her busiest and most exciting years, 1958–1968. You won't find every detail there, but as I listened she seemed to be in Vidal Sassoon practically every week for a cut or a comb-through; was constantly in sound rooms recording voiceovers for various products; and that was in between her actual work of acting! To help stir up old memories we went on mini-pilgrimages to where she used to live in Clapton. We walked up to her old school and the caretaker gave us an impromptu tour. I think this trip led to The Clapton Flasher anecdote that appears in the chapter 'Clapton Child'.

Fenella was eighty-three when I met her and I wasn't really sure why she still wanted to be working, but then in May 2012 I saw her perform a reading of some excellent Greek translations at the Reform Club. She was in good company that night, with Simon Russell Beale also appearing . . . When I saw her perform, as I passed a packet of tissues along the row to the woman sobbing with emotion, shattered by Fenella's delivery in her role as Hekabe, I understood why she still wanted to work.

But the phone doesn't ring that much when you're eighty-three and you're not *actually* a dame. The offers of work tended to be invitations to sit and sign photos at conventions or appear in Q&A evenings, which was fun but not acting. As time went by, sharing Fenella's frustration I started to organise things for her. I set up her website, which has been an amazing way to connect to people who really do value her, and we set about doing our own things. We've made a number of themed internet radio shows together – things like gospel, jazz, cult TV themes and soundtracks. Great fun and well received. As I became the world's leading expert on Fenella's career, we set up our own 'An Evening With Fenella Fielding' nights. Our first was in Newcastle, my home town, where we had a full house (263 people) at the Tyneside Cinema. As we took the lift down to the auditorium I wondered what the hell I was doing. I'd never done anything like this at all. We walked into the auditorium and Fenella got a standing ovation 'just for being alive', she said. The energy was incredible. I think I just fed off that and the night went brilliantly.

Finally, we found a way to get Fenella on stage actually performing parts. I went back to the writer of the excellent Greek translations, David Stuttard, and asked him to write a two-hander for Fenella to read with Stephen Greif. Again, I wondered what the hell I was doing as I found myself producing one-off performances in the West End of our show *Just A Little Murder*.

The book had stalled, though. I'd present pages and Fenella would say something like, 'It's action-packed.' Which was clearly not an endorsement, so the book didn't progress from there at all.

In 2016, determined to get things moving, I put together some chapters not in a book form, but as a piece Fenella could read to an audience. We arranged the first ever performance at The Phoenix Artist Club that summer. It was a full house. Fenella was astonished by the reaction and still reminds me now about the audience's first laugh on the line about 'mental masturbation' (in the chapter 'Innocence ... Lost'); how they were hooked. We were hooked, too. We did lots of shows there – chapter readings followed by a short Q&A – as we honed what would become the audio book release in June 2017. The print book deal followed on from that.

We've spent so much time together since 2011. We've been to so many places together; even spending Christmases together with my wife's family. And all the time I've been collecting stories. You'll see what I mean when you get to the chapter 'Finale', and Fenella reveals what happened at the end of seeing *La La Land*. I had to put that in!

Fenella allowed me a free hand in structuring the book. Rather than presenting all of her amazing stories as a straight chronology running from the first to the last page, I have structured each chapter by theme. It's allowed us to approach what Fenella has always enjoyed in other people's biographies, 'the early struggles and early successes', from a number of angles. With that in mind, this book is mainly about the 1950s and 1960s. We agreed that it would be the best bits and worst bits of Fenella's life ... because nobody wants to read about the bits in between.

Fenella's recall of the past is incredible. Her telling is so colourful and what I particularly enjoy is the tenderness with which she portrays most (not all!) of the characters. It's this quality that makes the chapter 'Tarts and Gangsters' my absolute favourite. And what I'm so delighted about is how strongly Fenella's beautiful voice comes through, even in print. That's quite something.

Simon McKay, London, 2017

1

Clapton Child

When I was young we lived in Clapton, in the London borough of Hackney, in a small Edwardian mansion block. We had three bedrooms: one for my parents, one for my brother and one that I shared with a sort-of-nanny person. Nearby was the Venus Pencil factory with an enormous Venus pencil on its frontage. I took it for granted that it was full of pencils in the same way that the immense Christmas cracker dragged on by clowns in a pantomime finale was full of normal-sized crackers that they threw into the audience at the end of the show.

My brother Bas was three or four years older than me, so he got home from school a bit later than I did, which gave me a chance to sneak into his bedroom when he wasn't around. I'd been given a subscription to a worthy but boring read called *The Children's Newspaper*, but Bas had those exciting boys' magazines *The Hotspur* and *The Champion*, and I could read them fast before he got home, wallowing in the glamour of 'Dixie' Dale, the popular sports master, and the real horridness of Mr Smugg, a most unpleasant teacher forever doling out lines and punishing everyone in sight.

Bas didn't like anyone to read his magazines before he had, and he used to try to stop me doing so by hiding them. I remember one time when I invaded his bedroom: I searched and searched; I went under the bed. Nothing. I climbed up, looked in the wardrobe. Nothing. Suddenly I had an inspiration. My old rocking-horse was still in his bedroom. I pulled out the rocking-horse's tail, and there was *The Hotspur* rolled up with *The Champion*. He'd made an almost successful attempt to hide them from me, but I won!

Inspired by one of the comics I read, one day I decided to start a detective agency. 'OK, what are you going to call it?' someone asked. What we called it was the most important thing. We lived in Rowhill Mansions, so we called it the Rowhill Detective Agency. Then we went around looking for things to detect. There was nothing to detect, so it didn't last very long. But we did have badges; I made lots of badges saying 'Rowhill Detective Agency'.

I've got a lot of memories from my childhood because I remember everything – or at least I think I do. My brother doesn't. He says he doesn't recall anything before he was eleven. From what I've found, men don't remember as far back as women do, but it strikes me that either Bas is telling fibs because he doesn't want to discuss the past or else he's wiped out lots of memories without realising it.

We had some of the same teachers at school. He says he doesn't remember the one with the eyes in the back of her head, though he does laugh when I tell him the story about her: Mrs G.A. Jones, BA. We always wondered what the G.A.

stood for and decided that it was 'Gracie Araminta'. Before she turned away to the blackboard she would say, 'And remember, I've got eyes in the back of my head, so woe betide you!' I should think anyone who had been in her classroom would have remembered that 'Woe betide you!'

One memory that Bas certainly doesn't share is the Clapton Flasher – only I didn't know he was a flasher, or worse, at the time. One day, when I was about nine, I was coming back to where we lived. It was a mansion block, so a few families shared the same door to get into the building, then there was a kind of little lobby and stairs going up from there. Well, I came into the lobby one day and there was this chap with his back to me, and he turned 'round, he was probably about seventeen. He saw me and asked, 'Would you like to see me make milk like a cow?'

Intrigued, I replied, 'Oooh, *yes*.'

And there he was, in a flash, with flies undone. And in front of me was this thing, the like of which I'd never seen before, not even anything similar. And he asked, 'Would you like to touch it?'

'Oh . . . yes,' I said. And I put my hand on it. No sign of any milk, though, so growing bored I said, 'Well, I've got to go now. I've got to go upstairs.'

He said, 'Look, don't tell anybody about this.'

I said, 'Oooh, no.' And afterwards, of course, I told all my friends, who also didn't really know what it was all about. But I wouldn't have dreamt of telling my mother and father, because they just wouldn't have understood *anything* as interesting as that.

Of course it was terrible and that's why he was afraid I would tell somebody and he'd get into trouble. I don't know who he was. He didn't live there. Not in that block anyway.

Well, there you are. That's my first sexual experience, which meant bugger all. But what I love about it is my mind going back and forth thinking how I'd tell my friends, because they would love it, but not my parents because they would be too stupid to understand. If I had told them I would have had lots of 'forbiddings' – and then I would have known it had been something awful.

Going back further in time, when I was around two years old – or whatever age you are when you should be starting to speak – my parents were a bit worried because I was still speaking gibberish. But then one day they walked into the nursery and found me having a very animated conversation with my doll. I suppose I just didn't want to speak to my parents.

When I was about three I was taken, like many kids in those days, to an elocution teacher, where I used to recite poems. I can still remember the first one I learnt: *The Pillar Box*.

> *The pillar box is fat and red,*
> *Its mouth is open wide.*
> *It wears a tammy on its head;*
> *It must be dark inside.*
> *And really it's the greatest fun*
> *When Mummy lets me stop*
> *And post the letters one by one,*
> *I love to hear them drop.*

I also went to dance classes, taught by Madame Grace Behenna. My mother didn't escort me there very often. I had a sort-of-nanny girl, Miss Preston – I say 'sort-of' because she had no training – who was a beautiful nineteen-year-old with lovely red hair. She used to take me to Madame Behenna's by bus, and she would sit in class with the mothers of the other little girls. She had rather large eyelids, very cynical-looking, and as she watched the class she'd comment, 'Hmmm. Very hot. Very smart.' Madame couldn't quite grasp the sarcasm but she knew it wasn't a compliment. She told my mother that *she* ought to accompany me and not 'that girl'.

Madame Behenna really wanted results from the girls. She used to shout, 'Come on. Put a bit of pep into it!' But the most important thing was performing lots and lots of concerts, and I suppose that's where I first got the urge to go on the stage. Each year we would do a big show, and in the finale each child would be handed up a bunch of flowers. The mothers would supply them, of course, and to my absolute shame and fury all I ever got was a basket of artificial flowers – the same ones every year – while the other girls got proper fresh flowers. Not big, but real. Mummy always said, 'No, no, that's quite good enough for Madame Behenna, if you don't mind.'

Each child had a solo, as well as being in what Madame Behenna called the 'concerted items' – that meant the numbers performed by all the kids together. Every kid *had* to have a solo, of course, otherwise their mothers would have taken them away from the classes; but it meant the show went on forever. I must have been sound asleep by the end. I remember being in the show and then waking up in my bed the next morning, but never knew how I got there.

We did lots of other shows during the year, all at the same place. The grown-ups made it sound as though it was the London Palladium, but it was the Royal Northern Polytechnic in Holloway Road. I'm not sure it was actually 'Royal' but it was definitely 'Northern'. I was there with all my stage make-up on, and I can still remember the smell of the face powder. The shows were pretty awful, really, but exciting then; and after a while, because of the response, I realised I must be quite good at it. There's always some pleasure in doing something well.

Madame Behenna was always on the lookout for somebody who could do comedy. She was very high on that. She thought it was something I could do, so she had me do a number that was popular in pantomime, called 'Nobody Loves a Fairy When She's Forty'. I had to wear a kind of uniform: under my ballet frock I had long drawers with one leg longer than the other, each with different-coloured patches. My hair was in two plaits with wire inside so they'd stick out at odd angles. I had a fairy wand; the handle was broken and mended visibly with string, and its silver star was falling off. There was no mistaking it from the audience point of view; this was comedy.

Curiously enough, many years later in my lifetime of a career, I was doing cabaret at a gay club in the Fulham Road, probably in the 1980s, and during rehearsal the pianist said, 'I know a marvellous number you could do. I'm sure it would go down very well.'

'What is it?' I asked.

'It's called "Nobody Loves a Fairy When She's Forty".'

'Oh, do play it,' I said. So he did. It was full of extras and choruses, like panto numbers are. I mentioned it to a friend, the writer John Morley, who had been an actor when we met and played opposite me during the run of *Jubilee Girl* in 1956. I said how funny it was that my pianist had suggested this number, which I knew from doing it when I was little, and he said, 'Oh, darling, I know that number. Don't do it. People always think it's going to bring the house down, but nobody *ever* likes it. Don't do it.' But I suddenly thought, 'No, I don't think he's right.'

And when I performed it – to a gay crowd, because it was a gay club – they were helpless with laughter, especially when I sang the bits we'd added: 'Your fairy days are ending, when your wand has started bending,' and 'The glitter-dust they sprinkles, but it just shows up the wrinkles.' Now I know why so many of those 'Widow Twanky' men did this number in panto; clearly it's not quite the song I thought it was when I was a child taking classes with Madame Behenna. And I suspect that more recent interpretations might have come as a surprise to Madame Behenna, too.

2

Innocence... Lost

The less you know, the easier it is to get into trouble, even at school. I was fourteen and a half, fifteen at the most, and we were reading Rupert Brooke in class. It was modern poetry and very new at the time. A bunch of older girls came up to me and said, 'Look, there's Miss Scrimgeour.' (She taught English.) 'Go and ask her if she thinks that Rupert Brooke's poetry is mental masturbation.'

'Sorry, what did you say?' I asked.

'Mental masturbation.' They told me how to pronounce it. 'Go and ask her.'

I didn't hesitate. It was a literary question, Miss Scrimgeour taught English and would know the answer, and I was flattered to be addressed by sixth-formers, so off I went. As I approached her I could hear stifled laughter and hissed reproaches from behind me. Anyway, I did ask her and I have to say she was brilliant. She just said, 'I'm terribly sorry. I don't know what it means.' I didn't either, of course. The sixth-formers were all helpless and afterwards those swine had the nerve to ask me why I'd done it!

On the other hand, the more innocent you are the easier it can be to avoid difficulties. Some of my earliest stage jobs involved working in nightclubs for Cecil Landeau (I'll say more about him later), performing in revues. It was the mid-1950s – I'd have been about twenty-eight – and I found myself a cheap room to rent in Clarges Street off Piccadilly. I got the room through a friend, a painter called Denis Law who had taken me to the Chelsea Arts Ball. (Denis was a member of the Chelsea Arts Club and invited me to their annual costume ball at The Royal Albert Hall. It was full of painters, so it was very exciting really. As a costume, I wore Victorian underwear that I adapted myself with lace around the knee of the bloomers, and a camisole top with ribbon threaded through to make straps. Daddy reacted in the usual way, saying, 'Do you intend to go like that?')

I told Denis I wanted to run away from home to be an actress, and that the West End was such a long way from where I lived in Edgware that I wouldn't be able to get on with my career if I had to go home every night. Daddy had moved our family from Clapton out to Edgware in 1940, shortly after war broke out, as there was less risk of us being bombed – a wise decision, but rather inconvenient for me by this time.

Denis told me that he knew an art dealer, Ewan Phillips, who would rent me a room in his Clarges Street flat for two pound ten shillings a week. I rang Ewan up and he said, 'Fine, move in.' So I told my parents that I wanted to move out. They didn't react, maybe thinking that if they said nothing then nothing would happen. Anyway, my boyfriend at the time, Alan (who went on being a nice boyfriend for quite a while), came over to help me pack one Sunday when they were out. He put my suitcase in his car, and we drove from Edgware to Clarges Street, where Ewan lived with his girlfriend. We got chatting immediately. Then I rang home and said, 'You know what I said about moving away, moving out? Well, I'm there. I'm there now. I got there, so that's where I am.'

The morning after I arrived, Ewan came into my room with an enormous cup of tea. I'd never seen such a large cup. He put the tea down. I said, 'Thank you very much', and then he was gone. I sniffed the tea, which was probably lapsang souchong. It was completely different from any other tea I'd tasted. I hadn't come across any other kind of tea, just ordinary tea. This smelt vaguely smoked; it was almost bacony. I thought, 'Gosh, I hope I'm going to like it, because this is my new life.'

Now that I was in Clarges Street I could do this job at the nightclub without having to find places near by to sleep after the show. After the show we would sit in front and have breakfast at around two in the morning, and people would send over drinks as a thank you for the show. One night somebody sent me a glass of brandy, and the hostess said, 'He'd like to join you.'

'All right,' I said, and he came over and sat down. He was a dear little old man. Well, he may not have been a little old man exactly; he was certainly middle-aged, but at the time I thought he seemed rather old, and he was definitely little. We chatted away until finally I said, 'Well, it's been terribly nice meeting you. And now, I really must go.'

'How will you get home?' he asked.

'I only live round the corner.'

'Oh, don't be silly. How can a girl like you afford to live in the West End?'

I said, 'If you don't believe me I'll show you.'

He must have thought, 'God, you never know your luck!'

Clarges Street was a couple of turnings from the club. We walked along. He was a bit doddery on his feet. When we arrived at the house he asked, 'Do you really live here?'

I replied, 'Well, I have the key. Open the door if you don't believe me. I'll show you.'

'Fine,' he said.

I lived on the very top floor and there was no carpet, so it was clatter, clatter with heels – mine, not his.

'Well, there you are,' I announced. I showed him my room, which was little with some rather nice things on the walls and painted a lovely deep blue. It had a single bed and an ironing-board. He was absolutely charmed by the ironing-board.

He was teetering on his feet a little bit, and I said, 'Well, now you really must go.' And I moved him back to the front door and I opened it. He was still wobbling a bit. I said, 'Good night, it's been terribly nice and thank you again for the brandy.' And I closed the door. That was that. Nobody had ever looked as surprised as he did.

The next night I went to the club and I said to the girls, 'You know that fellow who came and sat at my table?'

'Yeah,' they said.

'Well, he saw me home. I showed him my room, and then I said good night.'

'My God. Did you manage to get rid of him?'

'Of course. There was no question of my not.'

One of them said, 'Well, all I can tell you is he would

have given you fifty quid if you'd walked on his stomach in high heels.'

It was unbelievable. If I'd known about that sort of thing either it would have come to a very sticky ending or I would have been wise enough not to take him home at all, but because I was completely innocent I got away with it.

Ewan's flat was extraordinary. He was an art dealer so it was full of paintings. And his girlfriend kept birds, so the whole place was full of branches and twigs and there was a great sack of birdseed inside the main bathroom door. I say 'main' because the bathroom had rather a strange layout with an extra little door, which I'd never really noticed until one particular day. I can't remember how long I'd lived there, probably not long. I was lying in the bath and this second door suddenly opened. In walked not only my mother but my Auntie Laura too, and they were both wearing hats. They had found me.

'Hello,' they said.

'Hello,' I replied, not sure what to say. 'Well . . . this is where I live.' I could see the sack of birdseed and the branches out of the corner of my eye, and the birds twittering near by. And there's me in the bath, which had legs like lions' paws; not considered charmingly collectable at that time, just desperately old-fashioned. Mummy sat down, very upright. I could see she was on the verge of tears. She kept looking at Auntie Laura, and Auntie Laura kept looking back at her as if to say, 'Huh, this is what she's come to. She's here!'

I can't really remember what happened next. I felt very vulnerable, because you would feel vulnerable naked in a bath, with the water getting cold, in front of two fully clothed people – even if they are related to you.

Mummy asked me what I was doing.

'I'm in a floor show at Churchill's, the nightclub.'

At the word 'nightclub' her face darkened. All she said was, 'Whose flat is this?' She couldn't take it all in.

I said, 'I'm perfectly all right. And I'm not coming home.' Finally, I grabbed a towel and stepped out of the bath. There was no terrible row or even a row at all – they went away, and that was that. It was extraordinary. My mother saw where I lived, but I don't think I showed her my bedroom, and I don't think I showed her the rest of the flat, because she just went back out of the weird extra door that I'd never noticed before . . . So that was them to the rescue, which of course I didn't need.

What was so good about living there was that Ewan liked me and we had lovely chats. One day I noticed there was a small painting, about twenty-four inches by sixteen inches, on the floor just leaning against the skirting-board,. 'My God, that looks like a Renoir!' I said.

'Yes, it is,' Ewan replied. 'I can't sell it. I paid too much for it, and now I can't make a profit on it because it's so small.' That meant he couldn't recoup what he'd spent on it, let alone make a profit. He always seemed to be behind throughout his whole career because of buying that Renoir.

Ewan told me about his girlfriend, and that she did a little work for the government. I got the impression it was for MI5 or the Ministry of Concealment.

'Oh!' I said, at a loss.

He said, 'Well, I do something of that sort myself. It's very easy for me because being an art dealer I have to go abroad a lot, and that's a good cover.' And he told me this and told me that.

Finally I asked, 'But listen, does that mean you're a sort of *spy*?'

'Well, yes, it does.'

'But if you're a spy, aren't you supposed *not* to tell me?'

'Oh, I know . . . It's just that I can't bear having to keep it all in and not tell anybody.'

'But how did they get hold of you in the first place?'

He said it had been on account of his girlfriend. 'Actually they've probably got a file on you as well because you're living here now.'

I was astounded.

Well, if they did have a file nothing ever came of it.

It was all sort of extraordinary. There were paintings everywhere; some were hung but lots were on the floor propped up against the walls. As you came in the front door you faced a spiral staircase. A wall curved round, and behind it was the kitchen. In there it was chaos. There was a wonderful charlady called Mrs Rudd, who was small and looked rather gypsy-ish, with very black hair. She would come in, take one look at the mess and announce, 'Well, I just don't know where to begin.' It was all very like that. And there was a great deal of cooking going on. That's where I had chickpeas for the first time in my life. I remember that as clearly as the first time I had sex . . .

I was still living with my parents in Edgware. I'd been to a wedding party in London and danced a lot with one particular boy. He knew I wanted to go on the stage – I was performing in youth clubs at the time – so he said, 'Why don't you come back to Oxford?' He was at university there. He said, 'The ETC (Experimental Theatre Club) is doing a show. You might be able to get some material.'

'What time is the show?' I asked.

'Seven-thirty.'

'But how will I get home?'

'We'll talk about that.'

'But where will I stay?'

He said, 'We'll think of something', and he did ... I probably twigged that it might involve a bit of sex, but in a way it was good because it had to be away from my parents. Quite clearly they wouldn't have let me go to Oxford if they had thought it was so that I could have sex – and I wasn't sure I would either. But also I *was* sure I would.

As I travelled down, I was very worried about what might happen later. I had packed my father's pyjamas. I thought, 'That would knock all allure on the head.' But it didn't make any difference at all; it probably added to it.

I sat there for hours brushing my hair ... well, probably not hours, probably not very long at all. I thought I might get away with it ... not having sex. But I didn't ...

Sex didn't seem to be anything in particular. Yes, well ... there we are. I went home the next day straight over to a friend of mine, and I told all.

3

Dragged Out of RADA

At first I didn't even know that when you were in a play you were meant to be at your place in the wings several minutes before you go on stage – not *just* before you go on. I would always be there in time, but would dash down at the last moment.

One day somebody took me aside and asked, 'Have you noticed that the cast are getting cross with you?'

I hadn't noticed. 'Why?' I asked. 'Am I doing it wrong?'

'No, you're playing the part beautifully, but they get terribly worried when you aren't in the wings.'

'I had no idea,' I said. 'I'm terribly sorry. Please forgive me. I'll never do it again.'

I really didn't know. I hadn't come straight from drama school. I'd been yanked out of drama school by my parents. I'd won a two-year scholarship at the Royal Academy of Dramatic Art, which was a wonderful thing. I couldn't have afforded it, and my parents never would have paid for it.

At first my parents were pleased and proud – a scholarship

is a scholarship, whatever it's for. But then it dawned on them that I was set on becoming an actress. When I was at RADA my mother would arrive at lunchtimes and try to take me away. It was unbelievable. She would say, 'Really, darling, these people ... these common people.' A few times she did manage to drag me away; other times she didn't. Nevertheless this all got back to the principal, and at the end of the year I was told, 'Well, sorry you've had difficulties. But you haven't carried out everything you should have done so we have to rescind the scholarship.' It was as if they thought I'd flung it back in their faces. So I spent one year at drama school instead of two.

I'm sure my parents thought getting me out of drama school was for the best, but how crass. They thought I'd go on the stage and become some sort of reprobate or harlot, that I would be fished out of the Thames, drowned. They just had these terribly old-fashioned ideas. Even their own contemporaries thought they were behind the times.

There came a time as I was growing up when I decided that I had to make up my own mind and see things from my own point of view. I made lots of mistakes because of that ... because not everything my parents said was wrong, but I got to the stage where I assumed that anything they said was bound to be faulty. That wasn't *necessarily* the case. Nevertheless, I wanted to close the door and find out for myself.

My mother came over from a small town in Romania when she was in her mid-teens. She learned English when she got here and became fairly fluent, but there were lots of words she didn't know. She couldn't read or write in English. She said she felt she was foreign. I'd often hear her speaking

Romanian on the phone to her sisters, although that might have been because she didn't want Daddy to know what she'd been doing.

She had a nickname for me, 'Finny', which was all right. But she spelled my actual name wrong, which led to the teachers at school calling me 'Finella'. I thought they called me that because they didn't like me. Child logic, but that can be very strong.

Sometimes, Mummy would stand in front of the mirror admiring her legs and say to me, 'Look, Finny, I've got beautiful legs. You must always tell people I've got lovely legs.' But it made me terribly worried. I didn't know when to say it. Should I wait until people asked, 'What are your mother's legs like?' And then I could say, 'She's got beautiful legs'? But it never did come up in conversation, so I'd like to mention it now. My mother really did have lovely legs. There. That's such a relief.

My father came from Lithuania. He arrived in England when he was eighteen months old. His parents couldn't speak English, and he had to leave school at twelve to help his father in his butcher's shop. He was terribly bright and a terrific reader. He did well in the end.

When I was about three years old my father was managing a cinema in Silvertown, east London. I remember being taken in somebody's arms to the cinema; great big faces on the screen. And I got the impression that Daddy was important there because I was presented with a coconut square covered in chocolate that was very glamorously wrapped in gold tin foil. Later on, he ran a ladies' underwear factory. When I was ten I was taken there to be impressed. If he'd had a normal upbringing and a straightforward education, God knows what he could have been. It is remarkable that the world has changed so much; he wouldn't have been able to leave school at such a young age now.

Home life was horrid. Daddy used to knock me about with his fists, and my mother would egg him on. I thought it would pass, but it didn't, not until I told him that if he did it again I'd report him to the police. I think that made him realise what he was doing was wrong, but it's hard to feel affection towards someone who hits you. In public, though, he had bags of charm. There's a saying, 'street angel, house devil', and that was him.

He was a Freemason and the head honcho. He made wonderful speeches at the lodge, and they all thought he was terrific. Mummy used to say to me, 'They should see him at home when he's telling us off and having a shout!' There are people like him everywhere.

My father didn't have any patience with me. He thought, 'It's all very well for her. She's had things easier than I did. I had to go out to work and earn a living.' He would say to me, 'You've had all this education. We've given up all these things for you and made sacrifices.'

Mummy said the same. 'We've made sacrifices.'

I didn't understand this. I said, 'But Mummy, I got scholarships everywhere. I got scholarships at little school and later to go to my proper school and finally a scholarship to go to drama school.' But that's not what she was talking about. It's the kind of thing that disappointed people say to younger people. Parents can be very resentful of their children having more opportunities than they had. When I told Daddy *maybe* I wanted to go to university, he said, 'I'd rather see you dead at my feet.' It was extraordinary, so melodramatic.

My mother took it for granted that she wasn't well educated. I think she thought it was rather feminine. She had married Daddy and she was very proud of him for being so clever, but she didn't like me having too much education, although she was pleased that I went to a very good school. I think that sometimes people are afraid that their kids will get uppity with them, which teenagers are apt to do. Every teenager has two or three years of rolling their eyes at their parents.

In the early 1950s (I can't recall if I had done any little revues at theatre clubs or not by then), an actress said to me, 'You should get yourself into a concert party that runs for a whole season and you're doing everything – sketches and songs. It's such an experience to do something like that over and over again eight times a week.'

I was intrigued.

She told me to get in touch with Hedley Claxton, who put on concert parties in seaside resorts like Yarmouth and Torquay. So I got myself an audition. I did it. He very politely thanked me for my time, and then I never heard from him.

I thought, 'Oh dear. He said he'd be in touch, but I'm obviously no good and I'm not going to get anywhere. I can't bear the idea of going on like *this*.'

Things were being a bit grim at home, so I was jolly miserable one way or another. I thought, 'I'm going to kill myself. That's what I'm going to do. I'm sick of it all.'

I went to Boots, and bought a very large bottle of aspirin. I didn't know what else you could take. I took the bottle home and sat on my bed with a glass of water in my hand. I took, in the end, about seventy aspirins, and I thought I would just sit there and die. Instead of which, all sorts of horrible things were happening. Suddenly I couldn't hear properly. (I think it's all the blood vessels near your ears or something.) I didn't feel good, and I realised it wasn't going to be a swift death.

I thought to myself, 'I want to die, but I don't want it to hurt. This is ghastly.'

It was the middle of the night, so I got up and went into my parents' room and told them what I'd done. I was very clear. I said, 'I want you to ring up the Boots that stays open all night and tell them what I've done – don't mention my name, but get them to tell you what I should do.'

That's what my mother did. Meanwhile Daddy was shouting. I couldn't really hear him because of the effects of the pills, but I could feel the vibrations from his yelling. 'Rah, rah, rah!' He was terribly upset about being woken up and God knows what else. Mummy came upstairs – I was in their bed by now. The man at Boots had told her I should drink mustard in warm water as it would make me sick. So I did that until I vomited up everything.

In the morning I felt really fearful, but I was still alive.

My parents called in the family doctor and told her what had happened. She asked how many pills I'd taken.

'Seventy,' I replied.

She said, 'Well, you can't have everything you want, you know.'

I thought, 'Bugger you. You don't know a thing.'

And that was that. I think she must have said to my parents, 'Don't talk to her about it. Just dismiss it from your minds and from her mind.' They never mentioned the incident to me afterwards, which was a great relief, but part of me would have liked them to have said, 'How awful it would have been if you'd died.'

That night I rang a friend of mine and asked her to come over, but she wouldn't. She must have realised I was terribly upset, but – this was really the key factor in whether or not she would come over – she said, 'No, I'm not coming over. I've taken off my tights.' I knew what she meant; once you'd taken your tights off, that was it for the evening. I begged her to come over because I was feeling so rotten. She wouldn't, so I went to her house, but I never liked her again after that.

The weird thing was, a few days later Hedley Claxton did ring me. He said, 'Look, I thought I ought to talk to you. I *do* think you're very talented. It's just that I need somebody at the moment who's a bit more experienced, but I decided I'd ring you and tell you what I thought. Because I didn't want to *not* ring you.' I thought that was lovely.

My parents just wanted me to get married. Clearly, I thought, 'Get married? I'd rather die!' People used to change when they got married; all of a sudden they'd seem matronly and middle-aged. That's all I could see. In the end, though, my parents did come round to my having a career on the stage. That's the weird part; after years of ghastliness, they came round.

It was 1958 and my mother had somehow discovered that I was doing something a bit out of the ordinary, a very unusual part. She turned up suddenly at a rehearsal for *Valmouth* in a hall that had been hired in the YWCA in Great Russell Street, coming in through the double glass doors nearest the stage. I think she was with my Auntie Laura. They were probably wearing hats.

I was in the middle of a scene and saying something I knew Mummy might take exception to. When I came off at the end of the scene, rather hurriedly, I went downstage and dragged her into the corridor. I said, 'Darling, you're not allowed to come into a rehearsal.'

She said, 'Oh, Finny, you're very good in this. Very natural.'

I said, 'I'm not natural! Natural is the thing I'm not supposed to be in this particular part.' But I knew what she meant. She meant, 'You look as if you're at ease doing it.'

She added, 'I've brought something for you.' And do you know what she had brought me? She had brought me a chicken, a roast chicken. And I thought, isn't that just like life? That's just what I don't need right now. When I wasn't working that's what I did need. But there it was. It was so sweet of her. It was almost like she was saying, 'Welcome back into the family.'

My father still had his objections. As a result of *Valmouth*, I had started appearing regularly on television. I did a spy thing where I played an Arabian girl in an oriental top and blue trousers, with a jewel in my navel. I liked the jewel so much that I visited my parents' house with it still in place. I showed it to my father, and he was furious. He said, 'I'm hoping to see you do something where you keep all of your clothes on!'

But things started to change with him later on. One time he came to see me on the opening night of *Luv* at the New Arts Theatre in 1963. He came backstage afterwards, and I said, 'Oh, Daddy, I'd like you to meet Murray Schisgal, the author of this marvellous play.' My father shook him by the hand, saying, 'And it didn't do you any harm having my daughter in it.'

He must have thought *Luv* was good because it was clear when he didn't like something. Michael Codron had put on a Joe Orton play, I think it was *Loot*, and during one of the performances somebody from the audience complained to the manager that the show was 'outrageous'. Michael got in touch with me: 'It wasn't your father, was it?' And you know, I think it was!

Things between my father and me were patched up to some extent eventually, but it took a lot of distance before we got to that point. It's so strange . . . Years later, I was home for the day and Daddy and I had a lovely chat sitting in the morning-room, as if we were complete strangers who had just met. Sometimes, how you meet somebody in life . . . you meet them on a bus, you fall into conversation, and it's as if you've always known them . . . and you find each other so interesting. We were enchanting each other. It was extraordinary. Then my mother walked in and said, 'Don't talk with your mouth full.'

I was indignant. 'Mummy, did you hear what you just said?'

'Well, you shouldn't.' She didn't mean any harm, but she spoke to me as if I were still a kid, while my father was talking to me now as if he had no preconceptions, no previous experience of me and was just taking me as he found me – and we got on very well. There was no grit, no nastiness.

It shows, the kind of war that had gone on between us all those years was not what he had wanted; it was not what I wanted either . . . I just didn't want to be beaten down.

My mother died first. She was seventy-five. My father lived until he was ninety-two and a half. In his last year, by which time he was living in a nursing home, every now and then in the middle of a conversation he'd suddenly ask, 'Have you been here before?'

And I would say, 'Oh yes, Daddy, of course I have. Lots of times.'

And he'd get an inkling that he'd said something odd and change the subject.

One day my niece went to see him. He thought she was me, and he was talking about all the shows I had done and said, 'I'll tell you the show I really adored you in. It was such and such . . . I didn't like that one, but I adored this.' I was very pleased when my niece told me about it.

On another occasion I was with him at the home, and I heard him say to one of the other residents, 'I bet you wish she was your daughter.' Things really had changed.

I gave him a T-shirt on his last birthday that said, 'I'm 92'. He never thought he'd live so long, but he did . . . And I *was* glad.

4

Enthusiastic Artistes Wanted

One of my first jobs came about when I answered an advertisement in *The Stage*. It was along the lines of 'Enthusiastic Artistes Wanted for Showcase Production'. It was at the Chepstow Theatre Club in the basement of a grand but rather shabby old house in Notting Hill. This had probably been the ballroom. Somebody had put in seats and a stage. When an advert says 'showcase' and 'enthusiastic' it usually means you don't get paid. You don't have to be that enthusiastic; you just have to want a job.

I went along to the audition with this boy, Geoffrey, who'd written a song called *Men*. It was a song I'd heard when I went to Oxford on the occasion I mentioned earlier that involved some sex. So I really did get some material to perform and I sang it here, initially without accompaniment, for the woman who'd placed the ad. She said, 'Oh, I know talent when I see it.' She was called Dolly Gwynne – very typical of a certain kind of stage name. She was blonde and although this was the fifties, her hair was done in a 1940s page boy and she wore a hat all the time. She engaged me on the spot, and it was to *be on stage* the following week. I got the 27 bus to Golders Green, then the tube to Edgware, screaming with excitement. I told the bus conductor, I told anybody who would listen, that I'd got my first job!

The scene shifts . . . it was the week of this great production, something like *Follies* or *A La Carte*. In the show was a woman called Madame Kate Opperman who was described in the programme as 'the celebrated South African soprano', but in the second half she occurred again as 'the celebrated South African contralto'. There were two dancing girls who were divine and they liked me very much and were very sweet to me . . . they knew I was a beginner. They wore black elastic fishnet tights. I'd never seen those before. They crocheted them themselves. There was a dancing couple called Alexis and Isolde. The woman was very thin. If she'd been a diagram you'd have seen where all the muscles join the bones. She wore a kind of Greek headband and tunic, and had bare feet. Alexis was quite muscular and he hurled her about all over the place; threw her around and ran to catch her. There was a conjurer and a pianist, Mr Vernon, who accompanied Madame Kate Opperman.

To get to the stage from the dressing-room you walked on some wooden planks laid over a kind of garden without any grass. The planks were very wobbly. You'd walk back and forth to the stage to do whatever you did. Madame Kate Opperman – this isn't going to sound true, nevertheless it is – well, Mr Vernon would come and consult with her before the show, and she would escort him back to the plank footpath, then . . . she would pick him up in her arms! She carried him across and then backstage. This must have been so his black patent shoes wouldn't get muddy. She was a very strong woman – amazing. I was frightened of her, really. Somehow it came up in conversation that she'd had all of her bosom removed – I suppose she must have had cancer or something. I said, 'Oh really?'

She replied in a booming voice, 'Yes, if a thing offends you, cut it off!'

Madame Kate Opperman had a repertoire that was rather amazing. I can't remember what she sang when she was being a contralto, but when she was being a soprano she sang rather saucy flirtatious songs; very much posing, finger-in-the-cheek kind of songs. She wore lots of rouge, as if it was plonked on. (I'd see her in the dressing-room before she went on and she looked quite different, wearing little gold-rimmed glasses.) Then she went on and did this song; it was Scottish, called 'Whustle and I'll Come Tae Ye, Ma Lad'.

I had two numbers in the show that were both written by two boys at Oxford University. One of the boys, Geoffrey Spain, actually came and accompanied me each night, with never a thought of asking for money. He was so sweet. Before we opened, which was the next minute, I'd asked Dolly Gwynne , 'Are we getting paid anything?' She replied, 'Oh no, no. This is a showcase.' Which is what I'd thought anyway, so I wasn't too put out. Besides, I felt one ought to suffer for one's art and this *was* a kind of suffering, not getting paid.

Then the most amazing thing happened. Lots of agents came in that week and several of them made a great approach to *me*. I suppose it was partly because I was so young, and I think possibly because of the kind of material I was doing

– which was rather sophisticated, whether I did it well or not. One of the agents – this is an extraordinary thing – I recognised her! She didn't remember me, but when I was a kid I went to her dancing classes. Mummy used to take me on the 38 bus to the West End. It was New Oxford Street or somewhere nearby. She was called Madame Ida Lille, which doesn't sound real but lots of people who taught back then were called Madame something or other, not just their name.

There was another agent, Tony somebody, who was very keen and wanted to get me to do cabarets in hotels in places like Bournemouth. I said, 'But I haven't got the material. There are only these two numbers.'

'Oh, you can work up some other numbers,' he said. But I didn't.

I did, however, slowly build up my repertoire to include a number written by Stanley Myers. He came along and played for me at some of these huge auditions at places like the Dinely Studios on Marylebone High Street. They used to be absolutely jammed with performers and a few agents. The acts would come in wearing full make-up and costume in the daylight – and stage make-up used to be much stronger than it is now. It was bright orange, with tons of rouge and blue eye shadow, scarlet vermilion lipstick. Sometimes they would be the kind of acrobatic acts where they got thrown about or did the splits or very high kicks. Stanley Myers was a menace at these auditions because he'd get the giggles. I'd say, 'You'll have to go out. You can't sit here and swallow it. Go outside or we'll never get any work.'

The next thing I did was work backstage at Bolton's Theatre

Club in Drayton Gardens, South Kensington. I answered an advertisement for that as well . . . 'Enthusiastic Students Wanted For Theatre'. The word 'student' meant unpaid, too.

I thought, 'This looks wonderful. I'll apply.' I'd read loads of theatre books and autobiographies, and I distinctly remembered that in Ellen Terry's wonderful autobiography (I was madly in love with her, although of course she was dead) she spoke about her work in a drama school in Barnes. I thought, 'Oh it must be like that – just what I read about. What will happen is . . . ' And it was all made up in my head before I even went along. In the morning we would do voice production, fencing, that sort of thing. And in the evening we would be *privileged* to walk on supporting distinguished actors and actresses in whichever play they happened to be doing.'

Of course it wasn't anything like that at all. What it was . . . I was an unpaid dogsbody. Lots of people were lured along by the ad, although many left the moment they realised there was no money. Of the remaining people – quite a few because people are always very keen – it was found out who was experienced in working backstage. Then the stage director – the uber-boss backstage – selected two people to be the ASMs (Assistant Stage Managers); they were to get thirty shillings a week. The rest were to get nothing. They'd do anything: sweep the stage, find props, prompt, run out and buy sandwiches for the actors . . . and I was one of those. I was nevertheless thrilled.

It turned out that they had a good director and got very good actors to do what looked like very good plays. They opened with a light comedy, *Here's To Us*, with a marvellous American actress called Helen Horton and an actor Robert

Beattie, who was quite well known at the time. I was on the prompt book during rehearsals, and I had no idea how to do it. They'd be making a stab at it, like you do, and I would suddenly call out, 'Oh no, it's nothing like that at all, you've got the line completely wrong.' Instead of the director shouting, 'Sack that girl', he just shrieked with laughter. Everybody whispered in my ear to tell me, 'What you say is such and such.' It was lovely being forgiven like that.

Then they had a play called *Lady Susan*. Dinah Sheridan was the leading lady; she did lots of movies. It was an adaptation of a Jane Austen novel, with a very good cast. I was made understudy to all the leading parts, but of course you don't necessarily go on.

The next play was *The High Bid* by Henry James, which was preceded each night by the one-act play *Still Waters*. Jenny Laird played the unhappy sister-in-law in *Still Waters*, and when she had to be off for a week, as I was understudy I had to go on. It had never occurred to me to learn the lines! I just loved the title of being understudy. Nevertheless, I did learn them very quickly and did go on for a week. And I know they were pleased with me, from talking with people who had spoken to the director. I had long hair then so they didn't even need to hire wigs for the period stuff, I could just put my own up, so they saved money on wigs.

By this time I was an ASM and I was getting thirty shillings a week, plus six shillings for selling programmes before the show, which was all very thrilling. I knew that obviously they weren't going to give me whatever Jenny Laird's fee was, but I thought they were bound to give me a little something because they were so pleased. Instead of which, not only did they not give me anything for appearing but they actually deducted six shillings because while I was in the play I couldn't very well sell programmes as well! And I thought, 'God, that's terrible ... not nice.'

So I went and saw the stage director and said, 'Listen, they've done this. What do you think?'

He said, 'Darling, I know it's awful and they shouldn't have done that, but the fact is there are so many actresses in London, all over the place, who'd have done that part willingly for nothing, just for the chance to be seen. At least you still got your thirty bob. That's what it's like.'

I thought, 'Yeah, well.' It wasn't that I was greedy for money, far from it, but I thought, 'I'm not going to stay here much longer. What I really want is not to earn a fortune but simply to know that they chose me because they thought I was good.' Recognition.

Nevertheless, taking the part in *Still Waters* was my first feeling of being professional, and a lot of people did notice me. There were two boys in the company who told me that I ought to get an agent. I didn't know how I'd do that, but I heard somebody who had seen me, Al Parker, had spoken about me to the director. He was an agent, a great big American, and I'd once worked for him in his office as a shorthand typist. (I'd not been brilliant as a shorthand typist.) Anyway, he'd noticed me. One of the boys said, 'You ought to make use of everything that happens to you, every possible help.'

And so I rang up Al Parker. I said, 'I believe you were there to see the play when I was on as an understudy, and that you mentioned me to the director of the play that night. I was wondering if I could come and see you.' He replied, 'Oh yes, you've got dark hair. Yes, well, come and see me today. Be here at one o'clock.' I was in Edgware, which was the edge of London, so I thought, 'Christ.' I borrowed two shillings for the fare to go by tube. I went all the way from Edgware up to town, ran into Park Lane and tore into Mount Street, panting. Just in time. I sat down in the reception and had to wait for an hour.

When I went in, he said, 'Oh yes, oh yes. Remind me now. Yes, I did notice you, but look . . . this is my list of clients.' And he showed me his list of clients, who were all big stars: Michael Redgrave, Glynis Johns . . . all the people who were famous then, and some of them still are.

I said, 'But you asked me to come.'

He said, 'Yes, I did ask you to come. You know why? Because I never like to give people the heave-ho on the telephone.'

I thought, 'I wish you had.' And that was that. I got up and I said, 'It was awfully sweet of you to see me,' and I dreared off. It would have been ridiculous to make a fuss. It wasn't that he knew my work, but that he found me striking. Happens like that all the time until you make it.

Years later when I was starring in a play in the West End, people were piling into my dressing-room afterwards and there was this big American outside, saying how good I was and how much I'd improved and how much he'd watched me and so forth. I was inside and there were millions of people crammed in and I thought, 'Who is this guy? Someone who just wandered out of the audience?' I had the door open just a crack and I definitely wouldn't let him in, although I was very polite and said, 'Thank you very much.' When I closed the door, Margaret Johnston – a tall, beautiful and very well-known West End actress – said that she was married to the man who was outside the door ... Al Parker, the one I'd been to see all those years ago. She was helpless with laughter. She could hardly get the words out. She said, 'You wouldn't let him in!' And on a good day, that's what it can be like.

5

Tarts and Gangsters

I was living in Dorset Court, just off Baker Street, sharing a flat with this Australian girl, Toni Rees, who'd been a ballet dancer with the Borovansky Ballet. Then she'd come to London and put on weight. People often do that. They get terribly skinny when they go to somewhere hot like Capri, but the moment she hit England she put on weight and then she couldn't get a job in the ballet. Something must have happened – she got married, lost the lease or something like that – so I needed somewhere else to live.

Somebody told me about a jazz musician called Dave Wilkins, who was going on tour. He was living in Adam's Row and he wanted to let out his room while he was away. So I nipped over to see it. Adam's Row was just divine . . . a mews right behind the Connaught Hotel, really in the heart of Mayfair. They were tall, thin houses; they weren't big. This house belonged to a man called Eric Turrell. He didn't live there, but he let out all the rooms to different people; an amazing mixture. One was a very posh girl who had a very high job as a very posh secretary. One was a young woman who was a shorthand typist, but also very posh. One was a man, Neville Croft, who'd been an actor and was now in advertising . . . and the Queen Bee of the place was Sheila Wood. She was a tart, but not a straightforward tart. She was voluptuous, bordering on fat. She didn't count herself as a tart because she didn't stand in the street. She was a hostess at Churchill's nightclub.

Churchill's in Bond Street is where, every now and again, I appeared in Cecil Landeau's nightclub show. But I didn't get to know Sheila until I came to live in Adam's Row. She was fascinating. She more or less ran the joint. She had the best room, which was on the ground floor, near the front door. She had the best room because she paid the most rent. She was earning a jolly good living from being a hostess. Also, I think she was the one who paid the char, Mrs Goddard, a divine Welsh woman who came and cleaned up the place as far as could be managed. The house was just round the corner from where I was doing cabaret at the Don Juan in Brook Street. I could walk to work! It was lovely. Dave was lovely, too. He told me I had a beautiful mouth. That cheered me up rather because then I thought I might be something after all, so that was very chirpy. And off he went on tour.

On the ground floor, as you came in from the front door, past Sheila's room, you went into an immense kitchen with a tiny kitchenette at the end, which was always full of everybody's washing-up. It was unbelievable! Once a week Mrs Goddard did the washing-up, but the rest of the time we all just sort of piled it in there. There was an ironing board, always up; very useful. And terrible old armchairs that groaned and squealed, and sofas where you only had to lean forwards slightly and some awful spring would leap up and attack you.

Sheila had a routine. She would get back late from Churchill's – or maybe . . . 'business'. She would get up late, usually midday. That's when Mrs Goddard was allowed in. She would come in with a cup of tea to wake up Sheila and have a little gossip. Later, about lunchtime, Sheila's boyfriend would come over and then go again soon after. Then she would have a fitting in the middle of the afternoon. She had many dresses made for work. They were all identical. All low-cut sheath dresses, sort of mid-calf, which was the style then, and narrow wide-set shoulder straps, the ones that look like bits of spaghetti; each one in a different fabric. So the dressmaker would come round and fit her; pin her into another sheath dress, millions of them.

She went off to work about 8 o'clock in the evening. I think as a hostess you mainly had to be so attractive that the customers would want to sit with you, and she was really rather marvellous-looking. She was slightly overweight, but really and truly she did look like a young Simone Signoret. Fabulous.

One night, after one of my shows at Churchill's, I was home by myself. I went into the kitchen to make a cup of tea, sat down . . . and in came Sonia. Sonia was the band singer at Churchill's. She was very busty indeed and wore very tight clothes. She looked like a great big Victoria plum. Sort of overripe, about to burst and very mushy-mouthed, with blonde hair down to the collarbone. She had all this cleavage and very high heels . . . court shoes, matching her frock. I don't know whether people thought she was divine or not. I'd say, probably not. Well, she suddenly came through the door into the kitchen, and I said, 'Oh hello, Son'.'

'SHHHHH!' She really shushed me.

I said, 'Oh.'

She asked, 'Can you tell me where there's a tap?'

I replied, 'Oh yes, it's . . .'

'SHHHHH!'

In the end, I couldn't understand why she kept shushing me, but I managed to mime that if she followed my left arm and passed through she would reach the kitchenette where there was running water. There were two taps, hot *and* cold. I thought, 'What in the world is she doing here?'

Well, I heard the lot in the morning. Sheila was on rather hard times at that particular moment, no customers. But there had been one man who'd said that he'd really like to go to bed with somebody rather young.

'So', she said, 'I got Sonia.'

'But Sonia? Good heavens!' I said. 'Well, what was she doing in the kitchen? Why did she need the tap?'

'Well, I told her, "Go into the kitchen, wash every bit of make-up off your face. Tie your hair in bunches. Come back in, take off all your clothes, get into bed and keep your mouth shut".'

'So she was meant to be this young teenage girl?'

'Yeah.'

'Well . . . I mean . . . What happened?'

'Yeah, well, I hung around.'

'But did anything take place?'

'Oh yeah.'

'Yeah? But did he believe that she was a little girl?'

'Well, darling, you know how things are. I think he wanted to believe.'

Sheila was very nice and we got very chatty. She said to me one day, 'The other girls here, they all try to be like me. It's such a mistake.' I thought, 'Yeah, Christ, it is!'

She said, 'Don't you try.'

I said, 'Sheila, it would never occur to me, darling, really and truly. You mustn't feel that you would be responsible for me trying to become like . . . no, absolutely not.'

Well, she was rather exceptional. Quite a lot of her customers were regulars, and some fell in love with her. I know there was a particular American who used to put money in the American Bank for her once a week, whether he was there or not. He was mad about her. She wasn't just some dreadful old tart. It's funny, because I knew she'd been in a musical and when I asked her about it she said, 'Oh yes, I couldn't be bothered being on the stage. It's too much like hard work. Although the stage is an easy get-out from your working class.' But you see, her sister, who was also working-class and very pretty indeed, she didn't go on the stage nor did she become a tart. It's not a natural course of events that if you're working-class you have to go on the stage and/or become a tart – no, not by any means. I don't think what I chose to do was anything to do with class, not that I thought of myself as any particular class. I know I'm not working-class, that's a whole different life, or it was at that time.

The thing I did notice about Sheila was that because she earned pretty well, she was pretty extravagant. Perfume was very expensive even then, but she would sit at her dressing-table, with me there chatting to her while she got ready, and she would pick up . . . not a bottle of eau de toilette or even eau de parfum, but the actual bottle of perfume. And she would pour it into her palm, put the bottle down and just rub it all the way up her arms or on any exposed flesh. I've never seen anybody else ever do that. It was lovely stuff. It was called Carnet de Bal. I did try it myself, but it didn't work on me. Different smell.

The awful thing was that eventually she met an actor and she fell madly in love with him and he stopped her being a tart. Huh! He made her give it all up. He ruined her life! She gave me up, too. I wouldn't have minded but he wasn't anything in particular; he was only in an Agatha Christie.

When we were at the nightclubs men did approach us. But it was up to you to say no. And I thought, 'Well, I'm all right, thanks all the same.' Because of my upbringing I knew I didn't want to go nipping off with men I didn't know, just 'cause they'd seen me on the stage and fancied me a bit and wanted to fall into bed with me. I thought that was a terrible idea, that it would be the beginning of the end. And in one or two cases I saw, it certainly was.

There was this one showgirl at the Don Juan Club, she'd come from Nottingham to be an actress or a dancer. She just went to bed with anybody . . . anybody who had a word with the owner, Rico. He'd send them over, and she would trot off with them. It really was amazing. She went and shared a flat with some of the dancers, but they couldn't stand it. They said, 'She's so stupid! She's got no conversation and she brings back all these dreadful fellows.' And they asked me, 'Could you have her, just for three or four weeks?' I said, 'Oh, all right.' We were such good friends, so I did.

Well, she just was so stupid! In the 1970s, all round that time and a bit later, there was a sudden offshoot of feminism to go without a bra. Nobody did then, not at the time I'm talking about. But she would! She'd wander round the street at night, in a T-shirt and no bra, and then be amazed – terrified – if men followed her home. One night, I'd got back just at the right moment and she said, 'Oh dear, I don't know what to do. There's this fellow who's come in and he keeps taking the phone off the hook!' It was lying on the floor. 'Look, don't worry about it,' I said gently. 'But we really must have a little talk . . .'

There was a most beautiful girl at the Don Juan Club, called Bridget. She looked like a high-born German lady: marvellous features, very tall. To our absolute amazement she was a virgin, and she didn't seem set to lose her virginity. Anyway, she had this very strong Cockney accent, very honky. One night, she went off with some guy and everybody thought, 'Now, this is the moment!' So the next day, they asked, 'Well, what happened?'

She said, 'I don't know, I got very drunk, but he was a perfect gent and he didn't touch me.' In the morning she actually said to him, 'Good morning. I don't know who you are, but did I knock it off with you last night?' And apparently they hadn't because he was a gent and she was beyond drunk.

It was Bridget who came to see me when I was doing *Love for Love* at Windsor, while we were both at the Don Juan too. She liked the look of the male lead and she said to me, 'Tell that Patrick Barr that I fancy him strongly.'

The Don Juan was the most amazing place. The proprietor was Rico Dajou; I think he was Romanian. He was quite short, and he had the most distinctive hairdo I'd ever seen. His hair was grey and it was as if it all grew at the back of his head, at the nape, and he'd picked it up and wound it round and round and plonked it on top. It must have been down to his bottom when he let it go, but he did have it perfectly in place. Half-inch strands in ever-decreasing circles until it finished quietly.

It was very posh at the Don Juan. All the young male sprigs – offsprings of the nobility – used to go there; Dominick Elwes, son of the painter Sir Simon Elwes, was one of them. There was a sort of maître d' type called Charles who was always in faultless evening dress with a dinner jacket. He looked like a very handsome brute. Rico would sometimes rebuke Charles if he wasn't using the right terminology with the customers. One night Charles was tending to one of them, saying, 'Of course, your highness . . . Certainly, your highness.' Rico came up to him and ticked him off on the spot: 'Charles, Charles, what do you mean calling him your highness? Don't you know he's a fuckin' king?'

Rico got very cross with me every now and again because somebody particularly wanted to sit with me and I wouldn't agree. Because I was the leading lady he couldn't ask me to sit with a customer. It would have been lowering myself, and I didn't want to. I'd seen what it could lead to. When I was about fifteen, I was out with my grown-up boyfriend. (I say grown-up, he was five years older than me.) He was a journalist called Elkin Allan and my brother's very close friend. Bas didn't like the idea of me going out with Elkin, but I was very flattered. I thought, it's wonderful that he thinks I'm clever enough to keep up with him. It wasn't a deep, *deep* relationship, but I went around with him for a few weeks. He took me into this teashop that was not exactly Fortnum and Mason. It was 4 a.m. in The Coffee An', which was a caff in the Charing Cross Road. There was a tart there. She was a great big fat lady. She had very definitely dyed hair. And she was holding forth about the modern girl. She said, 'They come in 'ere, ladders in their stockings and their hair all over the place, and they've got the fuckin' cheek to call themselves prostitutes.'

It's fascinating, really, the people who were in the clubs and theatres. When we were rehearsing *So Much To Remember* at The Establishment, we saw men in the foyer who had those rather bent felt trilbies and belted camel overcoats, and we were a bit worried about them. The Kray Brothers, by this time, were an item that everybody knew about. These were not the Krays, but they were definitely gangsters. When I was actually doing my show, sometimes there was a particular table that was very talkative and I complained about it to Willy Donaldson, the guy running the place. He told me, 'These men who sit at that table . . . the only thing is, darling, they think you're terrific and they are the Nash Brothers.' So in other words, I'm not going to have a word with them about keeping quiet.

There was this story about one of the Nash Brothers, and I knew it could easily have been true because The Establishment was the only place in Greek Street – Number 18 – that didn't have to pay protection money. The story was that when The Establishment opened, while Peter Cook – who owned the club – was still in America and his business partner

Nicholas Luard was handling everything in London, one of the Nash Brothers came by to discuss an 'arrangement'. Nick spoke in a pinched voice and 'terribly laike that' and the Nash brother, whichever one came to speak to Nicholas, couldn't understand anything that Nick said. The Nash brother, all gruff and rough, 'talked terribly loike that', so Nick couldn't understand anything *he* said. And that's how, oh best beloved, The Establishment came to not have to pay any protection money at all, which I think is simply divine.

6

Cecil Landeau

Cecil Landeau deserves this whole chapter to himself because he was extraordinary. He had a tin ear for comedy, no idea at all, but if you did something and the audience laughed then he knew it was funny. I met him soon after my first backstage job. I did an audition for somebody who said, 'You're not really right for this.' But he gave me a number for Cecil, who used to put on cabarets, floor shows and, later, theatre revues that were quite famous in their day.

I got in touch with Cecil and he said, 'Well, come and see me.' And then I became one of Cecil's girls. I didn't know what was what. I had no idea. I remember the first time I was actually in the show . . . I had to sing a song called 'Jezebel'. It was ridiculous. I was leaning against a pillar, as if I was tied to it, singing, 'Jezebel-e-e-el, if ever a woman was born.' Etcetera.

Early on, one of the other girls took a look at me, grabbed my hair and put a rubber band round it. Ooh it was tight, I could hardly speak. They shoved me into some frock and gave me black fishnet tights. I, having just left Edgware, was still wearing a roll-on, which is what nice girls did then. It wasn't a corset but a sort of elastic girdle, so that people couldn't see the shape of your bottom. I was wearing the roll-on with suspenders and flesh-coloured stockings. I put the fishnet tights on over this thing and they caught on the suspenders and tore. There was such a row because fishnet stockings were so expensive, but also the girls were helpless with laughter. They couldn't believe that I was this nice girl wearing a roll-on and not taking it off before putting on the fishnet stockings. Anyway, that's how green I was standing there roaring out 'Jezebel'.

I had a thing about my looks. I went through a stage of being a bit of a podge, but nevertheless people seemed to find me attractive. Cecil Landeau really was the most dreadful man. He used to say to me, 'If only you'd be intelligent.' And I used to think, 'You don't know what you're talking about. I'm terribly intelligent.' He always used to try and find your weak spot, and one day he hit upon mine: 'After all, you're never going to be a glamour girl, are you?' So I soon had a lot of experience of putting up with Cecil.

The shows in Churchill's nightclub were lovely. Danny La Rue joined; he'd done something at the Irving Theatre before, but he was still unknown. Cecil Landeau always had the most beautiful girls in the world in his shows, but nobody was as beautiful as Danny La Rue because he really had something extra. He had real glamour and he went to an enormous amount of trouble putting himself together. Well, I suppose you have to if you are a man and you are going to dress like a woman. He wore black fishnet tights with flesh-coloured tights underneath, so if he had hairy legs it wouldn't show, although he did actually shave. He was gorgeous and he kept attracting the audiences.

The two men who ran Churchill's – Harry Meadows and Bruce Brace – they had a row, so one of them broke away and opened a rival nightclub. It was in a side street more or less opposite Churchill's and he called it Winston's, very witty. He took Danny La Rue with him; he was like the leading lady of the shows, which was really marvellous.

The shows were very well written, but it's extraordinary what people consider witty when it's in a nightclub. I remember some number the girls sang . . . as long as you mentioned a name, it didn't seem to matter whose, you might be talking about anything, the Costa Brava or some beach somewhere. Every now and again there would be some apparently witty remark about some famous name – 'There's Eartha Kitt in shorts that don't fit.' And I thought, 'It means fuck all.' It was absolute rubbish, but people thought, 'Eartha Kitt. How brilliant.' Just for mentioning her.

We also did Cecil's show at other places: the Washington Hotel in Curzon Street (very posh); Ciro's Club in Orange Street, and the Mayfair Hotel. Eventually, Cecil put on a big revue in the West End and that was my first West End show. It was at the Saville Theatre, which is now an Odeon in Covent Garden. The show was called *Cockles and Champagne*. Cecil said, 'I'm going to pay you £12 a week for it.'

I said, 'Oh, and will you want me to sign a contract?'

And he replied, 'Now, you're not going to be difficult, are you?'

The idea of *Cockles and Champagne*, apart from having lots of beautiful girls in it, was that it would be a mixture of common and posh. Renée Houston was the common, this rowdy Scottish lady. Patricia Burke was supposed to be a bit of class. Pierre Dudan, the only man in a leading part, was romantic and handsome and French. Phyllis Neilson-Terry was in it, too; she was amazing. She was very tall, and you could see she'd been very beautiful. She was very much the old school of actress, like her elder sister Ellen Terry whose biography I so adored. She said to Cecil, 'If you can't find me a solo, there's no point in my being in the show.' When we had a coffee break I said to her, rather hesitantly, 'Oh Miss Neilson-Terry, I know somebody who could write you something because I've worked with him in a previous show.' He was called Miles Rudge. I introduced him and he wrote her a marvellous number. It was suitable to her age and her great height and her classy looks. It was all to do with being in Westminster Abbey. It was called something like 'A Shabby Abbey'.

Those rehearsals for *Cockles and Champagne* were unbelievable. Cecil never had any money, but he spoke well, dressed well – wore suits – and he was good-looking with rather thick wavy hair that made him look very reliable, but he wasn't. The girls were terrified of him. Rehearsals went on for weeks and weeks, really only because he didn't have any money. He kept losing the backers and having to find other ones. At a certain point, we'd all be called in to do a bunch of songs to a number of ugly men sitting in the stalls, who were obviously potential backers. Well, he must have got the money because we did go on.

All of the costumes in the finale for the walk down were

made of Nottingham lace. All different sorts, wonderful! And each dress was a different design. Although I was only new, not a star and only a little featured person, I had a marvellous dress and a separate bow at the end, to show off the dress as well as myself. Cecil had a wonderful line; he got all that material for nothing, just by talking to the manufacturers.

Rehearsals for West End shows back then used to be four weeks. If you were paid under a certain amount, after the third week of rehearsals you were meant to be paid a full rehearsal salary for the fourth week. (When Equity passed that rule, West End producers immediately started having only three weeks of rehearsals.) But at that time you could only get rehearsal money if you were earning under a certain amount – say £10. So Cecil would tell people they would be paid £10 a week, but when we opened he'd say, 'I simply can't afford to pay you £10. I'm going to pay you £8 and that's that.' Nobody ever thought of going to Equity to say anything about it.

I was friends with a girl in the cast called Pauline Johnson, who was rather tall and rather nice-looking – she was a singer. She had this marvellous thick hair parted on one side. It looked like Scandinavian furniture – I mean, that was the colour of it. She had this terrific voice, but she was terrified of Cecil Landeau. I was certainly very nervous of him myself, which was partly because he never seemed to understand anything anybody ever said – unless you were very confident, and then it was another matter.

I told Pauline, 'I've just read about these pills in the paper. They're called Oblivon and apparently they stop you being nervous.' She said, 'Oh, can I go halves?' So I went off to the chemist and got some Oblivon capsules. (They weren't on prescription.) We each took one before a very late rehearsal. I found to my absolute amazement that I was perfectly confident with Cecil and that I could make him laugh. If you're nervous and you have a thought in your head it never comes out right; but with this Oblivon ... I said something to him that I thought was funny, and suddenly he was laughing. Pauline wasn't scared of him either that night, so that was a wonderful discovery. That was the kind of man he was. You had to be very confident with him. Then he seemed to understand.

The running order of a show is terribly important. It can often make the difference between getting good applause and not getting much at all. Also, the running order has to work so that people can change costumes in time for the next item. Cecil used to spend a lot of time putting everything in the right order. He'd often do it before an evening rehearsal at the Saville Theatre, in Victor Valoti's café over the road.

Victor had one of those boards with sliding bits of wood with the menu items on them like 'Two Eggs and Bacon', 'Shepherd's Pie and Peas', 'Kipper and Eggs' ... all the dishes that he sold. What Cecil did was to write out the names of different items in the show and paste them over Victor's food lists. There was a song called 'Love Is Not a Flower, It's a Weed' and everybody shrieked when they saw it on the menu board! Cecil would be busy pulling out a number to move it further down, beneath something like 'Darling, They're Playing Our Song'.

Cecil picked people who were very talented, even in the

floor shows. But he somehow made it impossible for them to shine in the way they could, by not promoting them. Like Eleanor Fazan, who became a director when she got away from him. (She directed *Beyond The Fringe*, a Peter Cook revue with Jonathan Miller, Alan Bennett and Dudley Moore.) I remember we were doing Cecil's floor show at a Mayfair hotel and one of the audience said nice things to Cecil about Eleanor Fazan and he immediately said, 'Yes, she has improved and soon I will be giving her a solo number.' Of course, he never did. Diana Monks was a terrific dancer, Cecil knew that, but he always felt he had to keep people down or they'd become stars on their own account and he'd never get the credit. Diana got around it, though. She asked one of the choreographers, Paddy Stone, 'Can I be in this number?' And he said, 'Yes, yes, we'll do this with you and Frances Pigeon.' Then bit by bit, without Cecil realising, she got a lot of numbers in the show, so she stood out, which she wouldn't have done if he'd had his way.

In fact, there were a few of us who stood out in the show and got our names in the paper when it was reviewed. Miriam Karlin, she was there to do a lot of comedy; and Renée Houston was there to do a real lot of comedy. Renée's husband, Donald Stewart, was her partner in variety. That's when I realised how wonderful it was to have somebody who was a good feed. She was the twinkle, and I thought it must be awful for him. One day he was working just with us and I realised how good he was and how important what he did was. You see, you learn all the time. I'd only really been doing it a year and now I was in a West End show, so I had a lot to learn. Like how to get a round of applause in the finale . . . that's when we had to do a twirl to show off our frocks. I realised that when I got to the middle of the stage, if I did a smile – as if I just couldn't help myself – and then did my twizzle, I would get a big round of applause. So that's what I did.

I was in a sketch with Renée, supporting her. It wasn't of the standard I was used to in Fringe revues that were written by very witty people. These were in a different category. One of the laughs was when Renee said, 'Lulu? You look like a Zulu.' In that environment it actually did make the audience laugh. To my surprise, I also found that I was getting laughs on some of my feed lines. After a while, I noticed that I wasn't getting that laugh any more. I realised it was because Renée was doing something different . . . so I'd do mine in a different way and suddenly get the laugh back. She'd realise that and she'd do something else. I went through all of the things I could think of to keep the laughs, and when I got to the end of everything I could think of, I gave in. But it was fascinating, because she knew exactly what to do. When you know what you're up against it makes life harder, but also easier.

One night at Churchill's somebody had left the show and Cecil asked me if I had any cabaret numbers of my own that I could do. I said, 'Yes, if you like.' I brought a couple along, went over them with the pianist and did them that night, and they went down very well.

So the next night, before the show, he said to me, 'Very nice, dear, but you must articulate more clearly because I couldn't hear what you were singing about.' Instead of thinking he must be wrong because I got all the laughs that were there and you don't get laughs if people can't hear you, I thought,

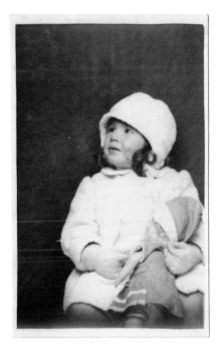

Top left: Fenella, aged about three. Fenella: 'I adore this, it shows a great sense of style in the days when you've got no choice about what to wear.' *Top right:* Fenella in Margate (aged about seven). *Bottom left:* Fenella in Margate, aged about five. *Bottom right:* Medals for Elocution, aged twelve or thirteen: 'I feel embarrassed being photographed with these medals.'

Top left: Cliftonville, Margate. Fenella, aged about seven. *Top right:* Fenella's father (Philip Feldman) as a young man. *Bottom left:* Fenella with her brother Basil in the garden of the family home in Edgware (Fenella about fourteen, Basil about seventeen). *Bottom right, above:* Fenella with her father in Edgware (late 1960s). *Bottom right, below:* Auntie Renée, Basil and Fenella (late 1960s).

Top: Fenella's parents: 'It's taken at an event because Mummy's got her diamond brooch on.' *Bottom:* Fenella with Juno Stevas in 'The Lift Girls' in a revue at Park Lane Theatre.

Top: Fenella's back garden production of *The Princess and the Woodcutter* (early 1940s).
Bottom: Local children stop by when Fenella visits a friend (c. 1972).

Left and Above: Playing Lady Parvula de Panzoust in the musical *Valmouth* (1958). This was Fenella's big breakthrough and led to everything.

Above: Vaudeville Theatre publicity for *So Much To Remember* (1963).

Left: Publicity still for
*Arrivederci, Baby / Drop
Dead Darling* (1966).

Below: Fenella did a lot
of promo work for BP
in 1967, which involved
personal appearances in
different towns around
the UK. This was in
Manchester.

Left: Fenella at her new flat in Connaught Place (1966).

Below: Beauty Fruit feature for *Harper's Bazaar* (1966). Fellini loved this series of photos and it inspired him to offer Fenella a major part in a film he was planning. She turned it down.

Top: Fenella at Scaioni's Studios, Marylebone (1959).

Left: Publicity still of Fenella with Patrick McGoohan for an episode of *Danger Man* (1960).

'Oh gosh. Oh dear.' And so I went on and all I could think about was articulating very very clearly. Well, of course all the laughs disappeared and I thought, 'You bugger. You bastard.' He just had to say something, whether it was true or not, so that I didn't get big ideas about myself. There are people like that in every field, who can see what you could do but don't want you to do it under their aegis. But if you get somewhere later on they will boast about you.

Audrey Hepburn was one of Cecil's dancers. She was a dancer in the chorus line of a musical called *High Button Shoes* and everybody noticed her because you couldn't not notice her, that lovely face; but Cecil was the one who actually went round backstage that night, and he got her for his floor shows and then for his revues *Sauce Tartare* and *Sauce Piquante*. That's where she became noticed. Then she got a tiny part as a cigarette girl in some movie and that led to everything. She went over to New York and she was on Broadway in *Gigi*. Cecil had warned her that films would be no good for her but soon she was in Hollywood and she did everything. Then Cecil boasted about her; how he'd given her her first chance and all that. Well, I can't help thinking that even if he hadn't, lots of people would have anyway.

Later, in 1967, I did a Henry James play at the Mermaid Theatre called *The High Bid* and it was fantastic for me. It really got me my straight acting badge; suddenly I was being taken seriously. I ran into Cecil somewhere. He hadn't seen the play, but he told me he was doing a musical and there was a part in it for me. He invited me over to his flat to see the script. I thought, he's going to offer me the lead because that's what I'm doing now, I'm playing leading parts. But it was as if he had never heard of me since I was a beginner in his floor shows. He showed me the script, and said, 'It's about a fashion house. It's called *The London Line*.'

I thought, 'Oh yeah, all fabulous costumes and about nothing.'

He said, 'And there's a nice little part for you.'

I said, 'Oh yes, who's going to play the lead?'

He said, 'Well, I'm thinking of asking Maria.'

'Maria who?' I asked.

'Maria Callas,' he replied. 'She's a very good actress, you know.'

Just a worldwide international opera singer, as if I would never have heard of her. I thought, 'I can't wait to see what she thinks about being asked to play the lead in a musical by Cecil Landeau called *The London Line*'.

I didn't feel up to saying, 'Don't you realise, you so and so . . .' Instead I said, 'Oh Cecil, what a wonderful vase of red roses you have here. Absolutely enormous, so beautiful.'

He said, 'Ah, they're from Audrey.'

'Really?'

'Yes, she sends me a great big bunch of roses once every three months. But, you know, she owes me a lot.' And I got the impression that really he thought she ought to be paying him commission on her fantastic career. As if he was saying, 'It's very nice to have roses, but what about the money?' And I thought, 'He's impossible, just impossible.'

7

Giving Up ... Twice

In 1952, Ron Moody was a mature student at LSE. He'd written a show to be done there, called *Cap and Gown*. (It was all about college.) A girl who was going to be in it had fallen ill. They had to have a girl to play opposite Ron to do sketches and songs. Even though I'd been dragged out of drama school I still wanted to do stuff, so I'd been doing amateur shows at youth clubs, sketches and songs. If I heard a song on the radio I liked, I would find out what key I needed and I'd do it. Somehow, one of the students had a friend whose niece knew a friend who'd seen me in one of these amateur shows and she said, 'I saw this girl. I know someone who knows her, and she'd be ever so good.' Ron said, 'Send her.' They got hold of me out of the blue so I said, 'Fine' and went along. I didn't have to audition or anything. They were lucky to get anybody at all. I suppose if I'd been terrible, he'd have just let me do very little. As it was, we seemed to be fine and I had to learn everything.

We were on for a week, and it gave Ron a good chance

to show himself off. One night, Ronnie Cass was there. He was the man who did all the music with Peter Myers and Alec Grahame; they wrote lots of revues for fringe theatres and they were casting another one. The awful thing is, I had auditioned for them two or three weeks beforehand. I was very inexperienced and I did a terribly bad audition in a tiny room. I did it very loudly as if I was in a big theatre, and I could see it was all so terrible and it was so embarrassing. I went away and tried to forget about it and then, to my absolute horror, a girl I met said, 'Oh, I know somebody who told me such a funny story the other day.' And that funny story was about me. So when I heard that Ronnie Cass had been in one night I wasn't terribly excited. I hoped he hadn't noticed me.

The scene shifts . . . ripple; dissolve . . . A few weeks after the college show, I was thinking to myself, 'I've got to be sensible. I haven't got any money. I've got to get a proper job where I get paid once a week.' So I went into the public library, looked at all the magazines and there was a thing called *Hairdressers Journal*. I turned over pages for adverts and there was a hairdresser who wanted a manicurist. I thought, 'Well, I can put varnish on nails.' It was for a hairdresser on Regent Street called Robert Fielding, and I made an appointment for an interview. I was going to see him at twelve the next day.

I got up in the morning, looked out of the window, but there was no view. There was nothing to be seen. It was all snow. It was Edgware, but Edgware had become Poland. Thick, thick snow. Bitterly cold. I thought, 'What am I going to do?'

You have to understand, when I say I had to wear my 'sheepskin boots', they were awful, not at all like nowadays.

You looked like a farmer with tree-trunk legs. But I had to wear them, and millions of jumpers and a big winter coat. The only nice thing I had on was a black silky fur bonnet. Mummy hated it, but I knew it made me look pretty. If anybody could look at me from the chin up, that was all right. So off I went, slipping through the snow to Edgware Station. I took the Tube to Leicester Square to find that Leicester Square was also Poland. It was absolutely thick snow except for bits where people had been treading, and that was terribly slidey. Suddenly, a voice came out of the snow. It said, 'Just the person I want to see.'

'Who is it?' I asked. And it was Ron Moody. 'Oh Ron, lovely to see you, what a surprise.'

He repeated, 'You're just the person I want to see.'

'Why?'

'Because I've got an audition this morning,' he said. 'Ronnie Cass came to see the show when we did it a few weeks ago and he's mentioned me to the others – Peter Myers, Alec Grahame and David Climie. They want to see me because Ronnie's raving about me, but they don't know what I can do.'

I said, 'Listen, Ron, before you go any further, I'm here because I have an interview to be a manicurist. I've got to be sensible, I'm not getting anywhere. That's what I'm going to do.'

He said, 'Darling, do come, please.'

I said, 'No, I've got to do this. I've got to be sensible.'

Ripple; dissolve ... That's how they do it in the movies ... the screen goes wavy and suddenly you're at ...

The New Lindsey Theatre Club, Notting Hill. I gave in because he said so much depended on it for him and it would make all the difference, so I thought, 'Don't be a bitch, do it.' I told him, 'All right, but you must understand, it was two or three weeks ago. I shall have to read it from the script.' I thought that if I had the script I could bury myself in that and they wouldn't be able to see me, but I'd be giving him the cues so he'd be able to show himself to his advantage.

We went on the stage. I took off my terrible sheepskin boots and stood there in my furry bonnet and winter coat, swollen out with my many jumpers, in my stocking feet. We did the sketches that we'd done at the LSE. Afterwards, they wanted to talk to Ron and hear him sing, so I just slunk off the stage and into the auditorium where I sat in the back row, trembling. After a while, I realised I was sitting next to a man. He turned to me and said, 'I was watching you, you're a very clever little girl.'

I thought, 'Oh.'

He asked, 'What have you done?'

I couldn't think of anything, so I said, 'Cabaret.'

And he said, 'Well, look, give me your phone number and if anything comes along I'll get in touch with you.' His name was Freddie Piffard, and it was only afterwards that I realised he owned the theatre. The show Ron was auditioning for, *Intimacy At Eight*, was already on in that theatre and had been running for six weeks. It was a terrific success, and the company had been offered the West End, to go into the Criterion. But while the show was still playing to good business, Freddie Piffard was legally entitled to keep it there, so what he did was replace each member of the company one by one to keep it going.

Ron was the first person to go in to replace somebody who had left. Later on, Freddie Piffard rang me and asked me to go in too. I was going in to replace Dilys Laye and do various bits and bobs. Anyway, bit by bit all the people were replaced, so it couldn't go into the West End just yet. It was reviewed again and we had terrific notices. It was the hottest ticket. Everybody came to see it and it was a great success. It was such a good thing to be seen in, and so much I did afterwards came from the experience of being in that.

Afterwards I thought, 'God, things swing on something so little', because that morning, when I woke up and found it was all snow outside . . . I didn't even know for certain that I'd get into the West End to go for the manicurist job. Supposing I'd left the house five minutes later or five minutes earlier, I wouldn't have run into Ron Moody and all that wouldn't have happened. So you see how destiny – or let's say just a little bit of luck – has to operate for something to happen.

Later, I was working out of town in a panto, doing three shows a day, but as the season went on and the audiences got smaller that dropped to two a day. That meant I was able to get a lift into London. While I was there I met my agent, Freddie Van Eyssen. He was on the phone to somebody else and he said, 'I'll just be a minute, darling. Nothing for you, it's just a new musical.' Afterwards I asked, 'What is this new musical?'

He said, 'Oh, there's nothing in it for you.'

I said, 'Why not?'

'You're too young for the part.'

'Oh, I'm not, I know I'm not. Well, what is it?'

'It's to play a Russian ballerina who is mistress to the

leading man. It's a musical called *Jubilee Girl*.'

'Well, why am I too young for it? I could do a wonderful Russian accent.'

'They want Maxine Audley.'

I knew who Maxine Audley was. She was this forty-five-ish, very beautiful, straight actress. I said, 'If that's who they've got in mind for the part, I'm not too young. I could play that.'

He said, 'All right, I'll get them to give you an audition, but I'm not expecting anything from it.' So I went back to Cambridge and did my pantos. The audition was arranged and I rang a pianist and we rehearsed the number I wanted to do. It was only when we got to the audition that I found out he'd been hired by the theatre to be the audition pianist! I'd already paid him, so I was a bit pissed off to find out he was playing for everybody else as well.

When it came to my turn, I was really a bit irritated by then. I walked on and I said to them, 'Look, I've been travelling all night and I've got catarrh up to here, so if you don't want to hear me sing I will quite understand.'

They said, 'No, no, we do want to hear you sing.'

So I did my number, and because I was a bit cross I didn't give a damn, and because I didn't give a damn I was jolly good, which is not a very easy thing to arrive at but that's what works. That's what worked for me anyway. They practically leapt on to the stage and asked, 'Are you free in June?'

I said, 'Well, I expect so. I'll have to find out.' They offered me the job and were terribly excited.

They had wanted somebody older, but they were perfectly happy to have me. They thought I was smashing. And so that's how I got the job. And it was all because we'd gone from three shows to two and I was able to be in London to talk to my agent and overheard his conversation.

I got wonderful notices for *Jubilee Girl*, but the show was a disaster; otherwise it would have made me, there and then. I had been so thrilled to get the part that I'd turned down an audition to do Shakespeare at Stratford-on-Avon. They were surprised. The woman asked, 'But wouldn't you like us to see you?' I really couldn't see the point, because I'd got this job and I started quite soon and it was such a wonderful part. And if I'd gone and done an audition there, they might have said, 'Oh yes, lovely' and I'd have been the female equivalent of a spear carrier, just doing an odd line here or there and having to work my way up. So I stuck with *Jubilee Girl*.

The show toured and did eventually come in. It played at the Victoria Palace, opposite the station. We did it twice nightly, 5.30 p.m. and 8.30 p.m. That was tough. It was a variety theatre, which was the wrong venue, and it was the wrong director: Casper Wrede. The first thing he took issue with was the opening number. He said, 'If you get applause for that then we're in trouble.' I thought, 'That's ridiculous, you idiot. If they applaud the first number they'll accept anything.'

What may have been my only chance had come to nothing, and I thought, 'Well, that's that. I'm not going to do any more.' Not much happened. I did this and that, whatever came along. I suppose it was two years later . . . I was living in a little flat in Paddington, in Eastbourne Mews, and I was very short of money. I hadn't got any prospects and the phone had been cut off. (Not because I hadn't paid the bill, there was building work going on and the cable had been cut by accident.) It was awful. I was kind of marooned. I was having the odd singing lesson, just to have a feeling that I was still in the business. My singing teacher asked, 'What are you doing, darling? Are you doing anything?'

I said, 'No, nothing.'

'Well, Sandy Wilson's doing a musical, you know.'

'Oh yes?'

'Well, he's a friend of yours, isn't he?'

I had met Sandy at a party. Then I went to a revue in which he had a number, and I became friends with him. He had a boyfriend called Jon Rose; I think that was all rather risqué at the time. He'd been at school at Harrow and took me to a cricket match where his old school team were playing in St John's Wood. (I had to wear a school cap!) I bought a song from him, and when I asked him what he charged he didn't know what to say so he said £25. I asked if it was OK to pay him in instalments, and he agreed. And over time I paid him.

I said, 'Yes, he is a friend.'

He asked, 'Well, are you doing something in that?'

I said, 'If there was anything in it, he'd ask me but I can't go and ask him, can I?' I sort of had a little weep and all my mascara went under my eyes and got all hardened, like mascara does when the black runs – it was all pulling. I left. Got home and I thought, 'Oh dear, just awful. Oh well, I shall just have to kill myself. I shall have to commit suicide. Well, I'm not actually going to kill myself, but I shall make myself some spaghetti, which will make me feel terrible.' So I started making some spaghetti and Bolognese sauce. Then a little miracle happened . . . the telephone rang. The cable had been mended and on the phone was Sandy Wilson! He said, 'Listen, how would you like to be in my show?'

I said, 'Oh, well I'd love to, Sandy. I don't really know anything about it.'

He said, 'Well come round. Take a taxi.'

I said, 'I haven't got any money.'

He said, 'Get a taxi. I'll pay at the other end.' Pay at the other end? That meant he was serious ... 'Come round now. I'll play you your numbers.' *Numbers!* Not *number.* So I took away the mascara from under my eyes and threw away the spaghetti and I got to Sandy's.

The part that he wanted me to play was one that I'd heard people talking about. It was Lady Parvula De Panzoust and it was a very important part. He said, 'Look, we start rehearsing in June. Are you free?'

I said, 'Oh yes, I think so.' I thought, 'Am I free? I'm free for ever, really. Name a date – I'm free.'

He said, 'Let me play your numbers.' He played me two extremely good point numbers. Point numbers are principally to make the audience laugh, and you're lucky if they've got a tune. These did have a good tune because they were Sandy's, and marvellous. They belonged to a situation; they weren't just out of the blue. He then played a trio number that I would be in, and that was lovely as well.

He told me about the part. There were three old ladies living in a mythical town called Valmouth. It was a magical spa town where people went to take the waters, and it made them feel young again. I would be the youngest of these three old aristocratic, posh ladies who looked fantastically young for being old, so you could see the confusion of it. Particularly as I was the naughtiest of the three and the other two looked on me as the baby. I just thought, 'Go along with it.' I went home in the taxi and rang all my friends on my newly restored phone and screamed with excitement, saying, 'I've got this job!' And I told them all about my part.

The horror of it was, though, the next day I had to audition for the director, Vida Hope, who was by no means sure that I could do it. She said, 'Oh darling, you've got such a young jaw line.'

I said, 'Yes, I know.' Because I was very young.

She said, 'It really ought to be somebody like Edith Evans who's got her own aura.'

I thought, 'Fucking cheek.' Nevertheless, I said, 'Yes, yes,' but I thought, 'I'll show you.'

Then she asked me my hip measurement, which I took as . . . 'You ought to lose a bit of weight.' That's when Sandy very sweetly stepped in, and he said, 'I'll read it with you. Darling, I know you can play this part. It's what you're like at parties when you've had a glass of wine.'

8

So Much To Remember

I've already mentioned that I adored *My Life* by Ellen Terry. In the early 1960s, when I was away in Guildford, I found a wonderful second-hand bookshop where I got some other theatre autobiographies: Constance Collier, Henry Irving. And the thing that was common to all of them: they made no bones at all about quoting stuff people had written about them or said about them that praised them . . . and a few bad just for a hint of balance. And I thought, 'God, it must be amazing to have the nerve to praise yourself in that sort of way, quote what people have written about you. Put it on paper.'

I was talking to Johnny Whyte, with whom I'd made friends in a terrible, *terrible* revue. We just sort of fell in love with each other. I mean, he was gay, but we really loved each other. We could always make each other laugh. I told him about these books, and I said, 'They always seem to have known people who invented things, and you get the impression that the Prime Minister couldn't move without having a private word with them. And the conceit about quoting all their good notices – Constance Collier saying, "I know I was in good looks that day."' He got the joke immediately, so what we used to do, just for fun, was to talk to each other over the phone as if we were these particular great people. We didn't use our own names. We used the names of people we'd worked with, other actors and actresses; people we didn't like too much. And this whole narcissistic thing was the joke of it.

We were laughing between ourselves somewhere and these two guys that we knew, Michael Barclay and Johnny someone, were there. They made records. When they heard us carrying on, they asked, 'What is it you're doing?'

We said, 'Oh, it's just a bit of fun. We're just taking the piss out of autobiographies where people are so keen on themselves and say so all the time.'

And they said, 'Well, do a bit.' So we did a bit, just made it up as we went along.

And they said, 'You know, that would make an awfully good record.'

'A record – oh, all right,' we said. We started to sketch it out and think of all the actors we knew who could play the parts.

All the conceit that you find in these people, especially the older ones, was rather bewitching. And it would all come out in innocent remarks: 'Now I have never considered myself a truly *great* beauty, but nevertheless other people did not share this view of mine.' That kind of thing. We did it in a very hackneyed way, which made the joke clearer. The opening lines were, 'I am not ashamed to say that I was born in Brixton. Number 22 Sunshine Street, to be precise, but nevertheless, many were ... And even as a child people thought ... ' And I talked about my mother in that wonderful way they always do.

It came from my idea, but Johnny Whyte put a whole script together. Obviously I would chime in with bits of things to say, but I couldn't have actually scripted it without him. It was a lovely collaboration. We had a sort of go at making a record of it, but the guys that made the records said, 'No, we were wrong, it doesn't really make a record.'

I said to Johnny, 'We really ought to do this live. I can't see the fun of just doing the voices anyway.' So we got Stanley Myers to do the music.

He said, 'Why don't we share this with Willy Donaldson?' Willy was a very decadent, funny man. Divine really, but totally unreliable, so Johnny showed it to Nicholas Luard instead to see if he might put it on at The Establishment.

At this time Peter Cook was in America with Alan Bennett and Jonathan Miller. They were doing *Beyond the Fringe* on Broadway. Nicholas had lost a lot of The Establishment's money on some theatre magazine he had promoted, so he was anxious to have a success. He read our script and he thought it was terribly funny, so we did it there.

I did the show with three boys: Jeffrey Gardiner, Bernard Lloyd and Mark Wing-Davey. They all wore shirts, V-necked long-sleeved sweaters and trousers – it was very unusual to wear everyday clothes at that time – and they added things or took them off according to what part they were playing. One of them played my mother, so he'd put something on his head and put on a bosom. Jeffrey, who was also a friend, played my lovable old dresser, who always said terribly flattering things about me: 'Ooh, she's amazing. She had the audience in the palm of her hand.' And this terrible conceit was what made the audience laugh more than anything in the world. At the beginning of the show, I was a little girl with my mother. She used to call me down from the nursery, to entertain my uncles. Uncles? They were, of course, all these terrible beery men that my mother was having it off with.

I wore a basic dress all the way through and used my own hair. But for playing the little girl, who was so talented that anybody would have been mad not to be able to spot it, I put on a wig with golden ringlets; it was obviously attached with elastic. I sang a song that was really rather saucy, except that it was sung by a three-year-old who wouldn't understand it, while everybody else did.

In the show, one day I was singing in the garden when somebody passed the fence and said, 'Ah, I hear birdsong.' It was Madame Italia Conti, who had a famous theatrical school for children, and she immediately gave me a scholarship and took me under her wing. And so it went on, until eventually I managed to cause the Second World War by refusing to give Hitler a complimentary ticket.

I'd somehow inspired, we said, 'Mr Edison Bell' to invent the telephone. It was installed in my home and rang immediately. I answered it: 'Mayfair 1'. And then, as the result of this phone call, I made a live recording of a big number in the musical I was appearing in. The audience all applauded when I'd finished recording it and I said, 'What a pity I can't be seen as well as heard!' And a man who'd been standing there listening . . . a light bulb went up above his head, and I turned to the audience and said, 'His name was Marconi.' It was all stuff like that.

The show was a big success. It was called *So Much To*

Remember: The Life Story of a Very Great Lady. We had to do it twice nightly. Then we transferred to the West End, the Vaudeville Theatre. And finally, we did it on BBC 2 Television. It was *quelque chose*. It was lovely to have had an idea you thought of yourself and it becoming something that other people found enjoyable.

In 1975 I'd just finished being in *Absurd Person Singular*, which I'd been doing at the Criterion with Paul Eddington. That transferred to the Vaudeville, but suddenly I began to want to not be in it any more. Partly because I was getting very depressed and Michael Codron, who was the producer, said, 'It's the play. It's what happens in the play. That's why.' The play took place in three different Christmases, and my character went from being very on top of everything to being this rather ghastly drunk. It was getting to me.

Somebody wanted me to do a couple of old-time music hall numbers at the Tramshed in Woolwich. They were offering me £250 a week, which was nothing. I told my agent to tell them, 'I'd like to do it if I can do the whole show. It will force me into putting a show together. The only thing is £250 really won't cover it. Music costs a hell of a lot.'

My agent said, 'Don't worry about that, I'll lay the cash out. If the show's good, when we transfer it you can pay me back.'

I started having a discussion with Billy Petch. I'd worked with him in cabarets and things. He said we must get together with Benny Green because he always has these wonderful ideas about very unusual numbers. 'Lovely', I said. It was basically going to be a one-woman show, but I'd need a partner on stage so I could do stuff I'd done in a revue with Stephen

Venaver at the Arts Theatre. Working with somebody gave more scope. I chose all of the things that I actually liked and decided that as long as I liked everything I could push them into an order of some sort and it wouldn't matter how diverse they were from each other. It would all work. It was a mixture of songs and sketches, which Billy Petch sort-of directed.

On stage at the Tramshed, I worked with this fellow Johnny – he was rather posh. We had a dancer called Bob something, and we worked out this smashing assortment of stuff. I called it *The Tramshed Follies*. People seemed to like it; we were there for a fortnight. Each day we took something out or changed the running order and got it just right. It cost a bit to pay an actor, a stage manager and some musicians (who were all very good), but I was secure knowing my agent had said 'Don't worry about the money'. Then he didn't come to see it until it was nearly over, and he didn't bring anybody useful with him. He brought another actress, very nice, but hopeless. He should have brought somebody along who might have wanted to put it on somewhere.

In the meantime he got me a commercial and said, 'Look darling, you've got to have some money.' I said I'd do it but it was a damn stupid commercial for Terylene, which I didn't like doing. Anyway, I did do it.

I then ran into Peter Diamond on a plane when I was doing a play up in Edinburgh and we chatted all the way home. Afterwards I suddenly thought, 'Well, Peter Diamond does the Edinburgh Festival.'

So I rang Peter and I said, 'I've got a thing I could do at the Festival if you like the idea.' So he came over. I was living at Connaught Place in Marble Arch at the time, and he only lived round the corner. I told him what we'd done and what the idea was – I had to make it up as I went along, really. He said he liked the sound of it and he offered me two late-night performances at the Lyceum Theatre. The Lyceum holds thousands and would be in the official festival. I said, 'Oh lovely . . . two nights . . . that's nice to begin with.'

The next day he rang up and said, 'I'll give you five performances.' It was to be called *A Personal Choice – Fielding Convertible*. Then the money was arranged and that was fine. I asked Bill Hayes to direct. He did plays, really, but I had seen him do a wonderful thing about miners and every now and again they'd sung. I'd thought he'd be very good. I talked it over with him and a fee was agreed, which wouldn't leave me with much.

The really awful thing was that when I'd first done the show at the Tramshed, I'd said to David, my agent, 'Darling, you must let me see the books', and he'd replied 'Course I will, darling', but he never did. He even got me to do a version of the show at the Watford Palace, but all the time he wouldn't show me the books. Then something awful happened. A cheque was returned to me and I was broke. I had this huge overdraft! My agent had withdrawn money from my account. I asked him, 'What's happened? You said I wouldn't have to pay you back until we got the show on.'

He said, 'Well, I'm sorry, my accountant says I must.'

I said, 'You know, I wouldn't have done the show if you hadn't said.' I still thought it would be OK. I said to him, 'After all, I shall be getting such and such at Edinburgh.'

He said, 'No, you'll be getting a thousand less.'

I said, 'David, you told me what the fee was for five nights, I'm certain of it. Why don't you ring up the Festival office and find out here and now?' He looked very unwilling, but he was obliged to ring them. When he'd asked them, he put the phone down and said, 'Yes, yes, you were right.' But what he'd tried to do was rob me of a thousand pounds, which is pretty awful.

Somebody had said, 'You ought to talk to him about the books before you go to Edinburgh.' But that was the wrong thing to have done because he was very angry about it. As a result he didn't send anybody up to see it. And it was such a success: we were absolutely sold out in The Lyceum, a great big theatre. So many people wanted to see it they had to open the gallery and the upper circle, which they hadn't done for years. Then we came back to London with this marvellous success and these incredible notices and nowhere to do it. We *didn't* go to the West End with it. It was such a wicked shame, but that was David's revenge for questioning him.

That was the last time I worked with that agent, but to make things worse I think he put out bad word about me. It was really difficult to get another good agent as a result of that. Anyway, I hadn't got any money and I'd got this terrible overdraft out of the blue. He'd taken everything that I'd earned, not just the commission, and spent it himself. It was just awful. So I was in a bit of a bad way; worse than a bad way. I had to put my flat on the market and move out. I went to live in Earl's Terrace, where at that time people stayed for joke rents of about £12 a week, I was told. The father of an old boyfriend of mine, the writer Tony Shaffer, owned the entire terrace so I went to see him. He thought he was doing me a terrific favour by letting me have a flat for *£38* a week, which seemed immense compared with what I'd heard from people who actually lived there.

It was hell. It really was hell. I had to go to the social security office and sign on. Getting up when my name was called was pretty ghastly. Well, I'm sure it's happened to others. I had to claim money to pay the rent . . . £38 a week outraged them. I can't remember if they paid it all or just contributed to it. I lived there for a year and then my flat was finally sold, but not for much. That just about paid for me to have a much smaller flat, but not in Central London. It was about 1981.

It was an arid patch, and I was reluctant to be interviewed by the press. I didn't want people to see how I was and write about me when I felt I was in such a bad way. There was no great turning point; things gradually came right and then I was doing a lot of plays, some very successful. I was about to go to the Chichester Festival and somebody asked me, 'Why don't you go to Peggy Thompson? She looks after people's money. After your agent has taken his percentage, he sends the rest to her and she banks it in a special account; your second account. All your household bills are sent to her and she pays them. So while you're away at Chichester for six months your phone doesn't get cut off because she pays all the bills.' It was a very good idea – and I've never had a cheque returned to me since.

9

1960s: The End of Deference

Everything changed in the sixties. People went around saying what they were going to do right now. People who ought to have been apprentices were talking as if they were bosses. Before that, people quietly nursed an ambition about what they wanted to do; but now, it was just extraordinary. Suddenly, skills didn't matter – or so they thought.

A particular thing about going into shops: shop assistants ought to have a good feeling about themselves, of course, but they don't have to put it on the outside in a defiant way. Some young people were behaving as if it was the last thing in the world they would do to be even decently polite to you. They wanted to show you they were equal, but they went too far. I came across it in various shops: girls with faces of stone daring you to be difficult; daring you to have the nerve to want to buy something. Nevertheless, I did know some girls of the same age who had been brought up beautifully. They were the ones who were going to get on. Things were changing, but they didn't change as rapidly as all that. You still had to have an ability, or if you had no ability then you certainly had to have bags of charm.

It was, I think, a misreading of what it was all about. It was as early as 1961 and very much to do with the influence of that television show *That Was The Week That Was*. People who had been venerated were suddenly shown up horribly, some of them quite unfairly. You couldn't say anything decent about anybody. Very important people were made fools of in that programme. Some of them were fools, but not all, but it was done as a matter of course. Ned Sherrin, the show's creator, said himself, 'It turned out to be the end of deference'.

The show was done at Lime Grove. Before it was launched, I went there at Ned's behest to meet David Frost, whom nobody had ever heard of. David was sitting next to Ned and he kept saying to me, 'It's so nice of you to come and see me today. It's so nice of you.' I thought, well, it's not really nice of me; I came to see you because Ned asked. I didn't know who he was. Nobody did. Ned had seen him doing cabaret at the Blue Angel nightclub and thought, 'He looks like the kind who would be very good to front this new show.' For one thing, David Frost was *not* good-looking. That itself was a slap in the face for the establishment. He had *not* a posh accent. The things he expressed were *not* his own thoughts, he didn't write the scripts, but over time he became associated with their whole thing: being very, very impatient with those in charge.

A lot of the 1960s began in the late 1950s. I remember a friend of mine, Sheila Green, went to apply for a job in a dress shop. Afterwards I asked, 'What was it like? Did you get the job?'

She replied, 'Darling, it was so peculiar. They only had a few things in the shop and they weren't anything like you see in marvellous shops like Selfridges or Harrods. I'm sure she's going to go down the drain.' And she was talking about Mary Quant, who had this tiny shop at the far end of the King's Road, next to Markham Square.

Talk about having brilliant ideas...Mary Quant knew what she liked wearing and what her chap liked her wearing. And she thought, 'If I do, lots of other people will.' They knew so little about the dress business that if they wanted to make a frock they actually left the shop and went to Harrods or somewhere and bought a length of material and made it from that. They didn't buy miles of it like you should or get it wholesale; they had no clue. But they had these very good ideas about what they actually did. They worked in the window. (There was no room anywhere else.) People would see them doing the making and come in and wait for them to finish the clothes; then whatever it was, they'd pay for it and walk out with it.

After a while some of her customers told her that they hated coming into the shop because when they came in from the street all the assistants were sitting along in a line all looking at them with faces of stone. They felt wrong for being there and sort of backed out of the shop again. Mary Quant thought, 'What?' She went in and had a look and she saw the girls doing it. They had a little signal among themselves and they'd look at the clients and decide whether or not they were going to serve them. Whether they were worthy of Mary's clothes! It was so ridiculous. Anyway, she saw them doing this and sacked them all on the spot and got in some middle-aged shop assistants who looked after everybody and let them try on clothes and buy them. So you see it wasn't just some conclusion that I'd come to. It was Mary who'd been such an innovator, protecting herself from bad assistants. She'd had this wonderful breakthrough and she wanted to stay in business.

Vidal Sassoon – he began in the 1950s too. I saw this girl in Mary Quant's shop who had this wonderful haircut. It wasn't Mary; it was one of her assistants. I asked her about it. She said, 'Oh, it's Vidal – a boy called Edward. But they're all marvellous, whether you have Edward or not.' It was Vidal who trained all his people so it was Vidal really. It was suddenly not 'off with their heads' but 'off with their hair'! I remember a particular photographer – Tom someone – saying, 'I really must do your photograph. I'm so glad you've got this wonderful new hairdo. Good! Good!' It was an extreme change: hair and clothes.

For an event, Vidal Sassoon took about six of us from his salon and he put a camera in each girl's hair. We all put on our evening dresses and caught a taxi to a West End cinema for the première of *I Am A Camera*. It was so ridiculous because we were meant to attract so much attention, but in fact a girl called Joy Berman, who had the most beautiful figure, got there first and everyone was photographing her. We hung around in the foyer but nobody took any notice of us at all. They were all concentrating on Joy. We walked into the cinema and watched the film, sitting there with cameras still in our hair feeling like absolute lemons; absolute fools! Nobody took any notice of us at all. So that was a stunt that didn't work.

In the 1960s, you had to go to Vidal – otherwise it was social death. Everyone spent their entire time having a comb-out or having it refreshed. Anybody who was looking for an actress to cast in a play, people said, 'Well, just go to Vidal Sassoon, you're bound to find someone there.' It was so popular. On New Year's Eve, when everybody had to have their hair done by Vidal himself, all these women were in his saloon. They were sitting all the way up the stairs, practically coming out into the street. They were all in tears, desperate to be combed out, terrified that he wouldn't be able to get to them in time for them to go to New Year's Eve parties. It was heart-rending.

On another occasion Peter O'Toole sat next to me; he was having his hair bleached for *Lawrence of Arabia*.

Now, think of The Profumo Affair: Christine Keeler, Mandy Rice-Davies. (Famously, when the barrister put to her, 'You are aware, aren't you, Miss Rice-Davies, that Lord so and so totally denies that you ever slept with him?' she replied, 'Well, he would wouldn't he?') . . . She used to come to Vidal's. One day she was having her hair done and a well-known duke's wife got out of her seat and went up to Vidal Sassoon and said, 'Really, Vidal! Mandy Rice-Davies in here, where decent women come to have their hair done.' We were all so ashamed. She was so awful. But the lovely thing was, Vidal didn't even look up. He didn't answer her. I thought that was marvellous.

The changes were everywhere. Photographers became celebrities: David Bailey, Lewis Morley and one of my favourites, Terence Donovan. There was a film in the 1930s called *The Threepenny Opera*. The photography in it is so extraordinary because everything is bleached out except the outline of people's features. Terence Donovan was doing photographs like that in 1961 or '62.

He did pictures of me. I saw some photos on his studio wall and I said, 'I wish that you could make me look beautiful like that.' (It was some model he had been photographing.) He said, 'I could do you and you'd be just as beautiful.' So he did. These pictures were amazing. I was living with Ken Smalley, who was in charge backstage at the Mermaid Theatre when I was in *The High Bid*. We sort of got together and in time he moved in with me at Connaught Place. We were together for a few years. When we broke up he simply moved out. Ken said, 'These are not so much photographs; these are works of art.'

Several were printed in *Queen* magazine. I remember Ellen Pollock, an actress friend, seeing some of them and saying, 'Darling, you're too young to have lines touched out.'

I said, 'You know, darling, nothing's touched out. It's simply a style of photography.'

Terence Donovan committed suicide. I remember getting in touch with him, and either speaking to him or leaving a message for him saying, 'I'd love to have another sitting.' Instead of him calling me back he sent me some prints and negatives of the old photographs. There was a wonderful one with a cat over my shoulder. He was doing stuff then that was very special.

Towards the end of the run of *Pieces of Eight* – so it was still only 1960 – I was sitting in the dressing-room between shows. I can't remember what I was reading, but it dealt partly with the 1920s and I thought what a marvellous time that must have been, when everything was changing. Then I suddenly thought, 'But that's exactly what's happening now.' It was amazing.

10

1960s: Stage Shows

I've mentioned that, at the end of the 1950s, I came very much to the fore in this extraordinary musical called *Valmouth*, where I played a part for which I was far too young; all the better for that, really. It was adapted by Sandy Wilson from a book by an extraordinary writer, Ronald Firbank, whom lots of people didn't know about. So it was very much a cult success. The same people came to see it over and over again. There was one woman, who must have been potty, who saw it forty-two times. She was a fascinating person, called Violet Wyndham. Her mother was Ada Leverson, who had been huge friends with Oscar Wilde. (She was one of the ones who didn't desert him when he went to prison and didn't cut him dead.)

I distinctly remember running into an English film director, Vivien somebody, and he fell on his knees in the street and kissed my hand. He said, 'I'd been meaning to come and see your show and I finally did because everybody said I must, and I've seen it every day now for the last two weeks.' That meant he'd seen sixteen performances, one after the other. It was a lot like that. Lots of people came to see it over and over again.

It was an amazing piece and I had an astonishing success that I had never foreseen, nor had the actual leading lady, Bertice Reading. She had *eleven* numbers; the show was written on account of her. I had two numbers and I was also in a trio, so I only had three numbers in total. Nevertheless, when it came to the walk down, the applause I got was unbelievable. The notices were amazing, too. It didn't seem to matter what I'd done before; this was what people now knew me for, something extraordinary. It transferred to the West End and ran there, too.

I went from doing *Valmouth* to doing a revue, *Pieces Of Eight*, co-starring with Kenneth Williams. There are two ways to become a star. One is to play a part that lots of people would be successful in if they had the chance to play it. The other is to do a part that very few people would be right for, and that was the kind of success I had had in *Valmouth*. Just a handful of people would be right for that part. It's not the best way to become a star because people always wonder what you're going to do next. It means that lots of things that might be open to you – that you have the *ability to do* – are not offered to you, because people think it's got to be something equally out of the ordinary. In a way I was lucky because the producer of *Pieces of Eight*, Michael Codron, was also the producer of *Valmouth*, so he knew what I could do.

Pieces of Eight was very successful and it made me more marketable, but it didn't have the stuff in it that I really wanted to do. That's why, very soon afterwards, I got myself a small part as Phoebe in *As You Like It*. (It was at The Pembroke

Theatre in the Round in Croydon.) I felt it was good that it was a supporting part because it didn't look like, 'Well, who the hell does she think she is?'

After that, I did *The Rivals*, also at the Pembroke. It was such a success. There had been recent productions of it in the West End, which had been nothing in particular, but this one got a wonderful reaction. People poured in. After the curtain came down, people asked, 'Have you rewritten it to make it more modern?' They didn't expect to understand every word of an eighteenth-century play. Actually, it's a fantastically domestic play; terribly like life. That's why it's so good. We just said, 'No, we haven't uttered one word that isn't in the actual script.' They came really to have a look at *us* but they were amazed that they actually had a lovely time and could follow the plot.

We got some notices that read along the same lines: 'We went to the Pembroke expecting to see a dusty old museum piece, but instead we saw this marvellous play with lovely performances.' Things nearly hadn't gone so well, though. I had a terrible accident two days before we opened. The cast were all over at my place rehearsing and I was in the kitchen making coffee. On a high shelf, there was a jar of turpentine with a paintbrush in it. It fell down and splashed into my eye, and burned it – awful! Nobody knew what to do. I was the only one with any common sense. I said, 'Take me to Moorfields Eye Hospital straight away.' They took me there about midnight and I had my eye washed out and a plaster put over to keep it clean. They gave me painkillers.

It made for a lot of publicity. The press came to the flat to photograph me with this plaster over my eyes. I was determined to go on. On the day we opened, I couldn't do the dress rehearsal but I was there anyway and the designer, Michael Young, said, 'Let me have a look at you.' The wig I was wearing for the part had some period ringlets. I wore a ringlet on one side and the eye patch on the other; I had one of those flesh-coloured patches from Boots. He said, 'Leave it to me. Let me have it.' And when he brought back the patch he had covered it in black satin with teeny-weenie lace edging. I wore this black eye patch with elastic in my hair and it looked wonderful. Absolutely marvellous!

We did a bit of rehearsal. I found the only thing was that if you have injured one eye it puts you off balance, but I soon got that back. Then when the play started, the moment I opened my mouth – absolutely full house – they wanted to help me and so began to laugh, and I thought, 'That is not a funny line. Not yet . . . Just go on, don't take any notice. Don't be influenced by it.' And I managed to quieten it so that they only began to laugh where it was right. I didn't play up to them. After two weeks I took off the patch – my eye was better – and finished the run without it.

The Rivals was a wonderful thing for me and it was a brilliant cast. I wanted, if it transferred, to go with it, but there was a terrible muddle about dates and in the end I was offered something else I had to do, so I wasn't available. Reggie Smith, a BBC radio producer, had said to me, 'You must continue with this piece if it goes on. It could change your whole career.' Only, in the end I couldn't. It would have been lovely to take that into the West End.

Anyway, later I did do *The Rivals* on the radio and this very *very* old actor, Baliol Holloway, who would go on to show Donald Sinden how to do an aside, was in the production

playing the hero's father. He said to me afterwards, 'May I say
. . . your Lydia is just the thing, the very thing! The best I've
ever seen.' It was such a lovely thing to have him say because
he'd seen so many generations of people doing the play. It was
very exciting.

My next stage appearance was in *Twists*, a revue, first at the
Edinburgh Festival and then at the Arts Theatre in London. It
was just the kind of comedy that I adore, and I didn't have to
tear my guts out like I'd had to in *Pieces of Eight*.

Later on, I did another play for Oscar at the Arts Theatre,
which was smashing. It was an American play called *Luv*, by
Murray Schisgal (earlier on I described my father meeting
him on the opening night). It was divine. Very unusual,
very funny. It had a husband, his wife and a man whom the
husband had known in that man's better times. I was the wife.
My husband was having an affair with somebody and wanted
rid of me. At the beginning of the play he's preventing the
other man from throwing himself off the bridge to commit
suicide. He's thinking, 'I'll push my wife on to this man and
she'll fall madly in love with him.' So he leaves me alone with
him. And the man is hopeless . . . dripping wet. Marvellous
dialogue. Really gorgeous.

You know how when you're a kid you send everything
up about the grown-ups? We were always talking about
our parents and imitating them. This will be very familiar
because it was used some years ago by Peter Cook and Dudley
Moore, now it seems quite ordinary, but we used to say, 'When
I was a boy – of course I'm talking twenty, thirty years ago – I
didn't have any luxury like nowadays. I got hauled out of bed,

beaten, washed in cold water, *if I was lucky!* Had to go to work, didn't have any shoes.' This play was like that. It had all of these wonderful 'our childhood' jokes. It was divine. As it was Oscar Lowenstein presenting it, all the intellectuals came. Doris Lessing, the novelist, came. That's where I met her and we became friends.

She said to me about my performance, 'Fenella, you don't know what you're doing on stage there. It's so marvellous.'

I thought, 'What does she mean, I don't know what I'm doing? I know precisely what I'm doing. I've chosen each thing that she's praised and decided to do it like that; emphasise this, throw away that. Even the way I stand. It's all worked out.'

What she meant was, 'It's amazing you've been able to play this part because we all know you're just a fun actress and here you are getting all of these very clever points in. I can't think how you've done it.'

Let me put it in one word. Patronising. Although she meant it kindly, it is the department of fucking cheek. But she did become a friend. She was lovely.

I have a history of getting into places where a woman wouldn't normally be invited. Jeffrey Bernard used to take me to the Colony Room, which wasn't actually a men's club but it was mainly men there. I wasn't a member but I got the feeling that it was 'If Jeff thinks she's all right, she must be.' It wasn't a soft lights and sweet music sort of place and there was a very tough, beaky manageress running it. Everyone sat at the bar, I remember. Francis Bacon was a member, and he liked me a lot. People used to sit there all day, just hanging out. Stage hands, waiting for it to be time for them to go to work backstage in their theatres. There was a piano there and nobody used it, so they gave it to me. It's still in my living-room.

I remember one lovely day at the Garrick Club – another club that didn't usually have women in it. I was always mad about the novelist Muriel Spark, and there was a tea party there to honour her. I said to her, 'Some of us think you ought to write a play.' What we didn't know was that she already had. The next thing was Michael Codron ringing me up because Muriel Spark had said that she was very keen to have me play Annie in this play she'd written, *Doctors of Philosophy*. We did it! It had a wonderful first act, really remarkable. The second act was not as good, but it was still Muriel Spark. The critics were quite tough about it. I think if it had been somebody unknown they wouldn't have been; they would have said, 'What a wonderful new writer.' But because it was her, they expected it to be totally perfect; perfect plus.

Codron and Muriel were so distressed. He asked her to do some rewrites, and she did produce some. All of us in the cast were very helpful, saying things like, 'I could stand here while so and so says this . . . and if that looks strange, I could throw that line over my shoulder as I'm leaving the stage.' Anything to fit in and make it work.

During rehearsals I rang Muriel to ask about something in the script and we started chatting. I said, 'Your writing is so note-perfect. It must take ages for you to write something.'

She said, 'No, when I write about something I usually get an idea for the title and then the book comes from that. And I walk about with it inside me for about three months. Then suddenly I sit down and type away. I don't leave the typewriter until I've finished.' The time it actually took her to write a novel was really only a few weeks, which is no time at all. She said, 'I've just thought of a title now: *Lord Leek's London Mistress.*' She never wrote it, though.

Anyway, that's what she told me about how she wrote novels, which was the last thing in the world I thought I'd get out of her. I asked if she did much rewriting. She said, 'No, once I've written in that way I might change a full stop to a semi-colon or an "and" to a "because", but it comes out more or less complete.'

Sure enough, when we got these rewrites to the play they were minuscule. They weren't things that could possibly change the shape or the effect of the second act or any act. It just was a couple of words or a small phrase. They were impossible. They weren't going to make any great difference to the fate of the play, and they didn't.

The critics had so much respect for her that they came again to see the newly refurbished play. They said, 'Yes, yes, but it still doesn't work.' And that was that.

Let's Get a Divorce in 1966 was a big step forward for me. It was a romantic comedy and also a period piece; a young wife with an older husband. She was all bored with him and had a lover. She said, 'Oh yes, we'll run away to the woods and live on nuts. If only there was a divorce law we could be together.'
In the end the husband was very clever. He suddenly says, 'Well, it's what you wanted; there is divorce now. The law has just been passed. I don't want you to be apart any longer. I give you my blessing.'

Of course she goes off and she gets bored stiff with this ridiculous lover and it all ends very happily back with her husband in some rather gorgeous, rather sexy scene. It's a lovely play, and it didn't matter it being done at that time instead of when it was first written. It was no longer very topical, but really it just means the grass is always greener. It was a very unexpected success and I got wonderful notices from all the top critics, which was very important for me. They could see that although it was a comedy it was also an understated thing. It wasn't all just lark, lark, lark and sending up. So that was a big break for me.

But the most smashing-est thing of all, my favourite thing, was when I played Hedda in *Hedda Gabler*. That was a *wonderful* thing and a lot of people rated it highly. I'd originally done *Hedda Gabler* on the radio in 1966 with Ian McKellen. It was on the BBC's Third Programme, terribly posh at that time. Charles Lafeaux directed it. He told us the story very well and I realised that although Hedda is a cow, she can be a sympathetic character if you play her right. Hedda thought, 'At my age, I should be married.' And you can assume she's pregnant, without making too much of an issue of it. Later, when I went to act at The Phoenix in Leicester, Robin Midgeley, who ran the theatre, had heard *Hedda* on the radio and he asked me to do it there, so I did.

In 1969 it ran for three weeks. It was just amazing, a wonderful play. Because Hedda is *such* a bitch, the effect on the audience was quite marked. If after the performance we were all in the bar, the people who had come to see the play were jolly careful with me in case I bit them. That's very normal if you play a part like that, your effect on the public. Many people were impressed, though, because they'd previously only known me for doing comedy.

I had a very worrying first night. The costume included one of those lace-up corsets. At the very beginning, before the play actually began, I came on in my underwear: a corset, a camisole and a petticoat. I was walking about looking irritable. The girl who made the corset had wanted to have a good look at it before the first performance. I shouldn't have let her. She took up so much of my time; she wanted to look at where it did up, where it needed to be tighter. It's all quite an art, but in the end I had to rush to get on stage. I had a huge pink corset lace trailing around me and it slightly fucked up Act One. But things settled down after that.

On another night, the cast was on stage and my friend Geoffrey Toone, playing Judge Brack, had to inform us of a death. He came from the back of the stage into the kitchen, in through a door that faced the audience. Then, what every actor dreads; the door handle – the whole thing, front and back – came off in his hand. He was left holding it. The audience didn't laugh. They didn't seem to notice but we, the cast, were helpless. We kept our backs to the audience; our shoulders were going up and down. We disgraced ourselves terribly. However, unnoticed by us, he simply made a detour from his usual route. The next thing, he was delivering his final line with great equanimity, nothing in his hand at all. Somehow, without anybody seeing, he'd managed to deposit the handle on top of the stove . . . and it didn't lose the mood at all.

Hedda Gabler was packed out. We were asked to go and do it at one of those smashing theatres in Scotland, but I was the only one of the cast who was free to do it. Such a pity. I think it could have ended up in the West End because it was so good and it hadn't been done in such a long time. Oh, agony. The fact is it is a wonderful part; a wonderful play. But nobody would have cast me in it except the guy who did cast me in it. Still, I did get to do it in Leicester for three whole weeks and that was fantastic.

Doing *Hedda* meant I got to end the 1960s doing something as wonderful as *Valmouth* at the end of the 1950s. And I got lots of lovely things in between. Lots of different types of roles, where I got to show that I wasn't just all larks; people got to see me in a different light. Some of the shows could have gone to the West End and would have done very well. But overall, I think I was jolly lucky.

11

Film Roles and Fellini

Rudolph Cartier offered me the part of a prostitute in a live television play on BBC in 1957, then he offered me something similar in a production the year after. He must have thought, 'She played a tart in that and we've got a much better part for a tart in this play, so let's get her for that.' All you can wish for is that six different directors think of you in a special way that is different from each other. One thinks of you as a tart; one thinks of you as a fine lady; one thinks of you as a pretty girl; and then you don't get typecast.

People are a bit shivery when they meet people who play villains or bad people. As I mentioned earlier, when I did *Hedda Gabler*, in which I really was wicked, if I ran into somebody from the audience in the bar they were very careful how they spoke to me. It's human nature. If you play a little darling, people come up to you and flirt with you. Any actor will tell you the same. If you're typecast as a great sex bomb it's very bad in real life because you get the wrong people approaching you.

It's a matter of vibrations. You know the kind of person who when they come into the room everybody goes, 'Uurmm.' Some people are drawn to it and some people think, 'Oh that's too much for me.' Or it takes them a bit longer and they say, 'I was quite afraid of you at first, but now I see what you are.' Well, it's quite hard. When you meet people, you have to show your real self. And if you play these larky parts people sometimes think that you might be able to get the better of them verbally. As though the wit that you're playing is something you've written yourself. Some people aren't afraid of that. Some people are attracted to it.

I was huge friends with Angus McGill. For years and years he had the centre pages of the *Evening Standard*. He'd seen me in something and really liked me in it, and when we met he liked me even more. We became great friends and he often used to include me in his column. One day he wrote, 'Fenella Fielding: the wittiest woman in London.' I thought, 'Oh my God, now I'm dead. If I just say, "Good morning" people will think, "Just a minute, just wait, this is nothing yet – just wait till she starts. You wait till she really starts".' So it becomes a huge responsibility, a burden, to be labelled in a particular way, even though it's a compliment. Can't I just sneak about? It can't have been true. It's just that he thought me witty because we struck sparks off each other. He would say something and I would come back with something, or I would say something that was only larky and he'd get it. But sometimes people don't get it. They might even take you the opposite way.

As long as I've been in theatre I've been friends with a lot of gay men. I think they felt then that they had a very hard time. Even now, there are plenty of people who put the knife in. But gay men seemed to feel that I would understand about the sex and not be shocked, and that I would understand gay humour. When you're in a show you can almost tell who's gay by who responds to parts of it in a very definite way. They tell you you're camp – they don't mean gay, they mean someone who understands them and their jokes. It's a particular sense of humour that's very hard to define. It's certain exaggerations and they know it's for a joke, not taking you literally. That's why people who can do 'camp' are very good in revue where you often do send-ups.

I was moving away from the revues and I had a part in a film! It was called *Sapphire*. I only had one scene, where I played a shop assistant in a fancy knicker shop. I saw it recently; I had a smashing frock. It was one of my own. I was lucky I didn't have to rely on what they could dig up.

It was my first film, so of course it was exciting. It was a *known* director, Basil Dearden. An actor who was waiting to do his scene said to Basil, 'She is going to be a star any minute now.'

Basil asked, 'What do you mean?'

'She's in this thing called *Valmouth*. It's going to go to the West End and she's going to be a big star.'

'Oh really, what is she doing here then?'

It was very strange. He probably hadn't been aware of me, maybe the casting people knew I was a name being bandied about. I think Basil Dearden was probably shown a photo by a casting agent and just thought, 'Yes, she'll do.'

I did the film *Follow A Star* while I was rehearsing *Pieces of*

Eight. The producer was lovely to me. He said, 'We thought you'd bring a little bit of Lady Parvula (that was the name of my *Valmouth* character) to this. It starred Norman Wisdom, and I was meant to be an upper-crust guest at a party. I wore a very low-cut dress; Norman accidentally spills an ice cube and it goes into my cleavage. That was the joke, so it wasn't exactly what you might call reminiscent of my role in *Valmouth*. I didn't think the film was going to be terribly popular. I was with a new agent by then and he said, 'Oh darling, if you do it nicely then you'll get lots of nice little things to do at Pinewood.'

'Nice little things?' I thought, 'Hmm.' But like a fool, I did it. It didn't put me in the right character at all. I remember the first time I saw Norman Wisdom – it was on television – I thought he was brilliant. After a while he developed mannerisms; a terrible thing of laughing a lot or crying a lot. I only had one scene with him, but I noticed in other scenes he'd be terribly good on the rehearsal but on each rehearsal he'd do it stronger and by the time he got to doing the takes he was overdoing it. I don't know if he thought he was overdoing it or if he thought he was doing it better.

Not a very pleasant man. Always making a pass – hand up your skirt first thing in the morning. Not exactly a lovely way to start a day's filming. Taking it for granted anyone was game. It wasn't confined to just me, of course. I remember Dilys Laye saying exactly the same thing. His attitude was: Female; fair game. No thought for, is he alluring? Are you interested? No matter. It was just, *ooo-er!* Female; go. Not very nice. And not the most attractive man in the world.

Foxhole In Cairo – I know I killed somebody in the end. What a terrible film! When it showed in one of Chelsea's King's Road cinemas, I got a round of applause for the death scene but I think it was a derisive round of applause. The thing is, I'll never know because some people say they like it. But at the time, when I was doing it, I was having two weeks of hell from Kenneth Williams in *Pieces of Eight*, crying my eyes out the whole time. It doesn't make you look too wonderful for photography. Also, there was a tummy bug going round. Not the best possible time to be engaged on a movie and not one I was even sure about. There was stuff in it that was taken from a previous film, extracted and incorporated into this film. Well, I don't know . . . if I were to sit down now and watch it, I might think, 'Oh, it wasn't so bad.' But at the time I wished I hadn't done it. And I wished that I hadn't been in that condition when I was doing it.

And then there was the fight scene with that ex-ballerina, Gloria Mestre. We knew we had to have this fight, and I said, 'We ought to rehearse it, oughtn't we? You do this, and I do that. And you go there; you jump as I do that.' It's always worked through, for film insurance if nothing else. They don't want you to break your leg or whatever. She didn't really want to rehearse, but when we did the take she went mad! I really had to *fight*. I had to call for help to get her off me! It was terrible. Bang! Bang! Crash! Wallop! It was *awful*! And you know ballet dancers are very strong; they don't know their own strength.

When Gloria first arrived at the studio, I thought, 'That is a very small nose.' And that always photographs well. Later in the shoot, when I went into the make-up room early one day, there was a row of soft noses all along the make-up table. And I looked at the make-up man, and he said, 'Yes, they go on her. We do a fresh one for each day. It has to be stuck on.' The story behind it was that when she was in the ballet in Mexico, it suddenly became very fashionable to have a nose job, so she had a nose job. And as many people do who've had plastic surgery, once it was done she thought, 'Hmm . . . that's better, but I think it should have been a bit smaller.' And then she kept having little refinements done to it, until suddenly it did look too small. So what they tried to do then was to restore it from other parts of her, to make it sort of all right again. All was well, but then one day, while she was out swimming . . . it floated away. And that was that, hence the row of noses lying on the make-up table.

Also, I know that she was very angry on the first day that I'd got a particular dress – it wasn't wonderful, but it fitted because I'd had fittings, I'd made sure of that. And she was furious. 'Why haven't I got a dress as good as that?' she demanded, and she had all sorts of rows on the set about my dress. From that, she sort of took rather a dislike to me. And I think that's why she whacked me. Anyway, she'd never acted before and she didn't know how you do those things. And that was that.

The Old Dark House was a Hammer film I did in 1963. There's a blonde girl in it, Janette Scott, who looks wholesome and safe. I'm the femme fatale. All the way through, you're meant to think I'm the wicked one, but it turns out that she's the wicked one. There's a scene where she comes at me with a knife. It was an extraordinary film – they decided to make it as a horror movie with comedy. So that's how it was done. We never had a première. There was a lot of delay about it, and when they did the rough cut they thought there was too much comedy in it. So they took a lot of comedy out of it and that didn't work. So they put it back in and took out some of the horror and they kept changing it back and forth.

William Castle directed it – he was lovely-looking. Ages later, there was that marvellous Polanski film *Rosemary's Baby*, which is the most frightening thing I've ever seen. I never go and see horror normally, but I did go and see that lots of times because it was so gorgeous. The bit in it that really made my blood go cold was when Mia Farrow suddenly realises what's going on around her with all of these charming old people – her neighbours, and even her own husband. And she manages to get out of the house, runs out and heads for a phone box and suddenly a man appears who wants to use the phone and she doesn't stand a chance. I thought, 'Oh dear, how awful.' Then I realised, 'That man is Bill Castle who directed *Old Dark House*.' He was probably on set that day and Polanski said, you go and do it for a bit of fun. And I was so relieved that it was only him, and for that moment, at least, she was perfectly all right.

In 1963 I was also in *Doctor In Distress*. I was a passenger on a train, and my hair was in a black bob. Somebody said to me years later, 'What a pity they gave you such an ugly hairstyle.' (Well, it's what everyone was wearing then.) I think if you behave as if you are ugly, everything about you becomes ugly, and I did behave ugly. The part was, 'Oh dear . . . oh dear, I'm terrified this man is going to touch me.' It was a nice part, working with James Robertson Justice. It was all right playing opposite him, but we probably had to do it more times than we would have normally because he tended to want to rewrite all of his own lines, which then means you virtually have to relearn your script. It wasn't dreadful or anything, although I believe on other films he really did use up an enormous amount of time. It was partly because he felt he was an educated man, and that if somebody had written the script who wasn't an educated man he was bound to be able to write better lines than they had.

Ralph Thomas, the director, said, 'He's such a pain, but the public adores him so we have to let him. That's that.' James realised he was very popular, obviously, but not how the filmmakers felt about him. It was Dirk Bogarde who told me. We were talking about that very funny scene in the first Doctor film about the 'bleeding time'; the bit when James Robertson Justice's character questions the students.

'Come on, come on . . . what's the bleeding time?' he asks.

'Half past three,' answers one of the students.

Dirk asked me, 'Do you know how long it took to do that scene?'

'A whole morning,' I replied.

'No.'

'A whole day?'

'No.'

'Two lines? Close ups and reverses and everything? A day and a half?' I said.

'Yes', he said, 'but we did have one more shot after lunch.'

That's incredible, but it did come out wonderfully. Very different to the *Carry On* films. They would never have allowed all of those retakes. They didn't allow any retakes unless the set blew up. From our point of view, at that time, the Doctor films were simply a cut above the *Carry On* films. (I'll tell you about the *Carry Ons* later on).

I didn't have a scene with Dirk Bogarde, but I met him when he was sitting outside his caravan between shots and he was most lovely. He chatted with me as though we'd known each other for ever. Later on, when I did my show at The Establishment, he came to see it and then he came round afterwards. I wouldn't have liked to have got on the wrong side of him, although I didn't know that at the time. He had his little ways, but he was lovely. Speak as you find.

Doctor In Clover was the most fun. It was fascinating. It was 1966 and I was playing a ballerina, Tatiana Rubikov. It was lovely being bundled off to the ballet to a rehearsal room to learn how to do the *Giselle* scene. Later, I met Wayne Sleep and he told me he was at the ballet school then. He said, 'Oh, everyone knew you were doing it and everybody came to the glass door to watch you.'

You know what's terrible in films, though? You do the master shot, but then you have to do the reverses and this angle and that angle. Well, with one particular scene in *Doctor In Clover* I did the master shot and it was the last shot of the day. A lovely thing happened – I got a round of applause from the crew. The next morning, first shot, to get the other angles, I had to do it again. It could never be the same.

The scene was with Arthur Haynes, who was lovely. I'd never seen him before. Judy Collins, a dancer friend of mine from when we were doing all the stuff at the Don Juan, she used to go off in the daytime and be a dancer in *The Arthur Haynes Television Show*. It was marvellous to come across him. His particular form of comedy was to be divinely exasperating: 'Oh, but . . . ah!' Every comic of that time had a particular thing, and he had those eyes. He rolled them in some way that I found very amusing. He was jolly good.

In 1966, I was in a film with Tony Curtis. It was called *Drop Dead, Darling* – or *Arrivederci, Baby* in America. In it, he was a fortune hunter. He married all these different women and then he murdered them, and kept their money. He murdered me, in fact.

Zsa Zsa Gabor was one of the wives. Another was Rosanna Schiaffino. I don't think there was anybody else, only me. So that's one Hungarian, one Italian and I was English. Being English, I had to be very posh and do horse-riding. Tony was actually a very good rider indeed. They needed to find a double for me – one with a 24-inch waist, I'd like to add. In the film, his character and mine would go riding together and jump over hedges. One day I was riding alone and jumped over a hedge, only he'd put it there at the top of a cliff, so when I jumped over it that was that. That was how he killed me!

As well as the films I did in 1966, I was also appearing at the Mermaid Theatre in *Let's Get A Divorce*. This boy I knew, called Neil, was to my amazement taking Federico Fellini all over London to see different actors and actresses perform. Fellini had come here to discover people. Neil took him to see a variety show, a film, an opera. And because Neil was a friend of mine, he brought Fellini to see the play I was in, which was having a huge success. Neil was taking him to see Act One of this play, Act Two of that play, so he was everywhere. Fellini never saw the whole of anything, just enough to get an impression. And he said to Neil, when he brought him to see my play, 'I like her. Can you help me get hold of her? Is it possible to do it without going through her agent?' Because directors always think about the money. So it was arranged that we meet in Claridge's. Fellini wanted to know everything. In the course of our conversation, he said, 'I saw you in that play, but you look quite different now. That amazes me. For people to have lots of different sides to them is interesting to me for my movies.'

Neil said, 'Come and have a look at Fenella's flat.'

Fellini said, 'Yes, I would love that.' So we went back to my flat, which was in Connaught Place, top floor. He was looking around at the paintings I had on the walls, the furniture and all that. He picked up some photographs. Ricci Burns, my hairdresser, had come over too and he said, 'Show him those photographs that Peter Deal did of you for *Harper's*. I brought up this big pile of contacts and a few prints. I could see him looking, turning over the first page of contacts, and suddenly you could see the exact moment when Peter Deal, the photographer, had suddenly got my point. Fellini could see that, too, and he was terribly excited. And the next thing that happened was that he offered me this film, which was to be the evocation of six or seven different men's desires. It was quite thrilling, really. He'd seen me in this play and these photographs, but not the films I'd done, and he wanted me to have this wonderful part that would show me off in so many different ways. Anyway, everybody was terribly excited.

The thing was that I had just signed to go to Chichester and do a season there. My agent said, 'I can get you out of it.' Everyone was saying that I ought to do the film. Then

Neil started telling me things about Fellini and the way he approached things – terrible things. He told me, 'People fly over, then the moment they get there he says he's changed his mind and he sends them back.' Stuff like that. So I began to get a bit scared and in the end I stuck with going to Chichester.

I don't know if I made a huge mistake. I'll never know. The things Neil told me really made me quite scared, that I'd be over there and it would become pretty nasty. Maybe he was exaggerating. I can't help thinking that perhaps it was Neil being a bit waspish, a bit spiteful. It seems to me now as if Neil was jealous, so he was implying that once Fellini got me there he'd find I wasn't as gorgeous as he'd thought I was. That it would all end in tears. Mine.

The film never got made. I think Fellini sold the script because he needed the money. About two years later, he brought some girl over – Beverly somebody, an actress – and he was raving about her. Suddenly it was all awful and she was sent back to England – not in disgrace, but she didn't do the film. It was awful for her. One minute she was like a new star, suddenly it was like she was nothing, and she's never been heard of since.

Well, everybody can make some stupid decisions and perhaps that was one of mine, but it doesn't mean my life is a tragedy because of it.

12

Television and Radio

The first time I was on TV, they were still doing it live. I was in a television revue with Dulcie Gray, who was, after all, a movie star. She and I were the two leads. And if you were out that night, you didn't see it. That was that. Everything was different about television then. Obviously we had rehearsals, but there was no telling quite how it would look. I still lived in Edgware. When I got home from doing it, my brother asked me, 'Why did you have to wear such black lipstick?'

I said, 'Well, I didn't. I wore very pale pink.' The cameras did funny things to you.

I mentioned earlier on that I did a spy thing on television where I was an Arabian girl who wore a top and blue trousers and a jewel in my navel that my father found so objectionable. I can't remember exactly what it was, but it had very beautiful women in it. And I was in a comedy programme with Tommy Cooper, twice, I think. I also did shows with Hughie Green and another with Roy Castle.

I had other television things betwixt and between *Jubilee*

Girl and *Valmouth*. One of them was a play directed by Michael Elliott, who was wonderful. It was a detective play, and I was cast in it because, from behind, I could look like another actress, Maxine Audley. This was important to the story because I was murdered when the murderer mistook me for her. It was wonderful. I had a dagger in my back. The blade didn't exist. What they had was the handle of the blade and two strings came through spaces in my dressing gown and were tied in front and underneath, so it looked as if I'd been stabbed. It was wonderful because I had to go to the canteen wearing it during the transmission. It was lovely sitting there with the dagger in my back, having a cup of yoghurt. I adored it.

Having done *Valmouth* made a big difference. It got me going in radio and TV and I really wanted to do more. A friend of mine, Kim Grant, said to me, 'You know what you ought to do: look in the *Radio Times* for the names of the people you haven't worked for and say, "I've just worked with so-and-so. I'd love to work with you". And ask them if they would please listen to this thing that you've just done.'

So when I was in *Valmouth*, before it transferred to the West End, I wrote to a director called Alan Bromley asking, 'Would you like to come and see me in this?' And I got a lovely letter back from his secretary, saying, 'Alan says to tell you that he has seen you in your show and finds you infinitely desirable.' The thing is, I didn't need to write to him to come and see it, and I thought, 'No more of those letters any more then.' So now, I've gone quite pink with shame. It sounds like boasting. Didn't mean it like that. But it was so funny for him to put it that way.

Something To Shout About was on the radio. It was about an advertising agency. Nothing like any advertising agency that's ever existed. Very good cast: Michael Medwin, Nicholas Phipps, Eleanor Summerfield, Joan Sims, Warren Mitchell and me. Warren was completely unknown at that time. Everybody else was known. Michael Medwin, he was very sweet because he didn't really have any discernible character to play, but he was so lovely in it that that turned out to be his character. He knew that the rest of us had got the plums and he was nice about it and didn't say, 'Oh well, I'm not going to be in it any more.' He stuck with it all through while we all had the best bits.

We used to do it every Sunday in the Paris Cinema in Lower Regent Street. We'd get there about 2 p.m., do a read-through, then we'd do another read with little elisions, excisions, alterations we were making for ourselves or suggesting. Putting in a repeat of a question, so that the reply would bounce back and be funny, instead of just being an answer, stuff like that. And also cutting out the odd word, so that the rhythm then made the line funny. Amazing the difference that made. (Later, I noticed that a bit in the sketches I did with Morecambe and Wise . . . it was the rhythm of them).

We did this every week as a matter of course, in the way that only people who are going to actually speak the lines can do. But we all understood what each other was doing. It was a very long-running series. One particular week the script was dreadful so we threw every trick that we knew into action at that second read-through. We did what we could, and then when we had to actually do it in front of the audience we did all the performance tricks we knew. Sometimes when something is a bit dodgy in its form you can improve it by the tone of your voice. It's like how they say dogs don't understand words, they understand your tone of voice – so we'd be getting a laugh at the end of that line when there was no real laugh there. And we went through the whole show like that with our alterations, and the delivery being paramount, just to save our own blushes. At the end, the audience applauded and I thought, 'But they didn't really enjoy it.' They'd hated it really, but it had worked. And I think it was the only episode that was below par.

I remember doing Hancock, too. An episode called *The Poetry Society*. I didn't enjoy it very much. When I arrived, Tony Hancock was at the mic and he just sort of turned round and said, 'Morning.' And that was it. Then Sid James, who was in it, came over and he was very nice. But Tony shook me a bit, so I just did it feeling I shouldn't really be there. Now of course I'm very glad I was in it, because it's still there and I still get tiny little residuals. You see, I wasn't to know that he was drunk. Well, you know by that time, he was probably hung over; 9 o'clock in the morning. Amazing he could do it at all.

I've done lots of shows on the radio. Lots of game shows – *What's My Line?*, *Just A Minute*, *Call My Bluff* – and lots and lots of radio plays. The radio plays always involved a few days' rehearsal leading up, and then it would be recorded, unless it was something frivolous and then it might go out live. In 1974 I did a Noël Coward play called *Present Laughter*, with Paul Scofield, and that wasn't frivolous at all. There were four rehearsals, then it was recorded. I was a guest of Roy Plomley on *Desert Island Discs*, too, and at the end I thanked him for 'my lovely desert island'.

I was a regular guest on *That Was The Week That Was*, which was a sort of current affairs television show with comedy and satire. The regulars on the show all thought it was somehow more thrilling to be a guest than to be in it every week. They had to work terribly hard and they were people who had special skills, like Millicent Martin. You could walk into a room, give her about ten pages of dialogue and she'd know it immediately. She had a photographic memory but she had talent as well. So she was very valuable. Anything topical that came in, they would write a number about it immediately and Millie would do it. Learn the music, learn the words and just do it! It was amazing. It was a great show to be in.

I had a lovely song on it once, called *Later Not Now*. It was a very sexy song. They had me doing it sitting on a television camera, which looked marvellous. The camera was in full view and then at the end of the song, still sitting on it, I disappeared upwards out of vision.

I'd just read a book of all the *Stories from Saki* when an offer suddenly came from nowhere to do it as a television series. Philip Mackie had had the idea and he'd got two writers together, Hugh Leonard and Gerald Savory, and got them to do the scripts from the book. He cast the main people in it and asked Silvio Narizzano and Gordon Fleming to direct; they alternated week by week.

From getting the idea to the day of the first rehearsal was only twelve weeks. That's brilliant. Philip Mackie *was* brilliant. And the plays were marvellous, just like Oscar Wilde, who cuts right through every single layer of humanity. The bus conductors liked it, the toffs liked it, the intellectuals liked it. It worked on all sorts of levels. When I got on a bus, everybody seemed to want to talk about it. Within three weeks of the series going out, we were number two in the lists for the most watched on TV – pretty amazing. We couldn't go to number one because that was *Coronation Street*.

In 1963, I was in *The Avengers*. Honor Blackman co-starred with Patrick MacNee, and it was one of the last episodes she did before she left to do films. There were rumours going around that I would be taking over from her. The press was so keen to find out if it was true that journalists kept taking me to lovely lunches at The Ivy and The Caprice. They just wouldn't believe me when I said I wasn't being considered for the part. The idea was crazy. In the episode I was in, I played a very scatty woman, nothing like the character they would need to be opposite Patrick MacNee. How could anybody think I was suddenly going to be transformed into this cool, adventurous, capable person with all that shooting, fencing, underplaying, to be suitable to take over from Honor? Mad. Although I wasn't completely incapable . . . my character's grandmother had had a knife-throwing act and, in a fight scene, I was able to throw a fencing foil into Warren Mitchell's back. Little did I know then I would have good cause to want to again later on in my career. (I won't bother going into all of that, but I will just say that I was in a stage play, *The Miser*, with him in the 1980s and he was horrible to everybody, including me.) Bloody good I hit him.

In my episode, *The Charmers,* I had a lovely scene where Patrick's character, John Steed, offers me a drink. We're in his flat. I say, 'Not before sundown . . . of course, you could draw the curtains.' They couldn't provide anything suitable for me to wear. Unbelievable. I provided my own costume.

Patrick MacNee always felt he ought to be doing fine things – not just things that were enjoyable for the public, but things where they might think, 'Oh, God, that's a bit much for me.' He felt that people who did the things that the public weren't so keen on were a cut above him.

A different Patrick: I first met Patrick McGoohan when I appeared in an episode of *Danger Man.* I was a nightclub hostess in that, he was the star. Later on he did *The Prisoner* and he asked me to be in that, too. It was like being the voice at a holiday camp coming over the speakers. It was terribly cheery: 'Get up. Go along.' Somehow it was so cheery that it was rather sinister. Patrick put his head into the sound studio before I did it, and he said, 'Don't make it sexy.' I thought, 'Mmm.' So I didn't. He was terribly nice. I did like him.

I played the title role in a Yorkshire Television show called *Izeena.* It was a terrible name. I was this girl in the jungle with very long hair. (Initially, it had been short but when Jean Hamilton came in as director she wanted the long hair.) The show was something about animals because it was in the jungle. Looking at me you couldn't tell that my character was supposed to be two hundred years old and getting younger each day. There were so many writers you never knew what style you'd be speaking in. Some writers write very long lines; others write very short lines. Robert Gould wrote the first ones, but it was too sophisticated. Well, it was a children's show! The rest were written by Robert Fuest. He'd been the set designer!

Each week, I wore completely different things. I seemed to spend a lot of time looking through a telescope to see all the animals in Africa, but it was filmed in Norwich. I do remember when I did the first one. My agent was very against it. He said, 'You'll get so fed up with it. It'll be like a millstone around your neck. You'll dread having to go up to Norwich every week.' He didn't want me to do something once a week because you become unavailable for anything else. And he was right in the end.

In 1970, I was in New York to do *Colette* off Broadway and I was asked to appear on *The Ed Sullivan Show*. He must have thought me interesting enough to have me on the show. I did a sketch and a song and I chatted with him. It was a very big show; I was just grateful to be on it.

The other huge show, not similar at all except in stature, was *Morecambe & Wise*. I made four appearances. I did two as the star guest in Eric and Ernie's play, and the other times it was popping on. They dressed me as a train guard and I had to say, 'I was on the *Morecambe & Wise Show* and look what it did for me.' It was wonderful to be asked to do it so many times.

They were lovely to work with. It's fascinating when you work with male comics – they usually want you to be good enough to show them off, but not necessarily good enough to show yourself off. But Morecambe and Wise were different. They did want you to show them off, but they wanted you to show yourself off, too. They wanted you to be ever so good, so they made sure that you had jolly nice parts. I loved the amount of detail in the work they did. There was no messing about. Eric was very technical, which of course is very good for comedy. He knew when to be sharp, when to do a punch line and when to be just crazy, just out of the blue.

Eric was definitely the boss, telling Ernie what to do. 'Not like that. Like *this*.' It was very thoroughly rehearsed. Often comedians don't because they like that feeling of being on the hoof, which gives you a lot of adrenalin. But Eric liked to know exactly what he was going to do, and he still had a lot of adrenalin.

The rehearsals lasted about ten days, which was quite unusual for that type of light entertainment show. Eric would get terribly fed up with certain lines, and just chuck them and ad lib something else, or get the brilliant Eddie Braben to write another line. Then he'd get sick of that. You could make another sketch out of the lines he cut out!

Eric was a great perfectionist about the little dance bits. And he loved if you could appreciate what they were doing. Having done lots of cabaret, floor shows and revues, I could appreciate what they were doing.

I've done Shakespeare, Ibsen, Chekov and *Dougal and The Blue Cat*. I didn't actually appear in *Dougal*, it was only my voice, but it was heaven to be in it; and quite a privilege because Eric Thompson, who wrote it, did all the other voices himself. I was doing *Let's Get a Divorce* and Eric (Emma Thompson's father) was in it playing a butler. We'd started off at the Mermaid Theatre to do it for just six weeks, but it was such a success that it transferred to the West End and had a very good run. Eric was going barmy because he was so bored playing this butler. He didn't mind doing it at the Mermaid but it was going on and on and on, and he had nothing much else to do.

Then suddenly, this *Dougal* came out of the air; it was a French thing. Eric's job was to translate it into English and make it suitable for England. He suddenly blossomed and made these wonderful scripts. I was the only one he brought in from the outside. I played the Blue Queen, so that was nice, telling people off!

In 2012, I was in the teen drama *Skins.* I was very pleased about doing this part because it wasn't comedy. I'm not saying there's no comedy in it, but this was a straight part and people could see I was being real. One of my lines in the script was a bit special. It got to be the last day of filming and I suddenly thought, 'Oh God, I haven't said that line, I wonder if it's been cut.' The line is when my grandson brings a girl home and says, 'This is Liv.' Then I look at her and say, 'She's a girl!' Because I know he's gay. And he says, 'Yes, that's right.' Then I turn back and have a look at her and I say, 'I like the colour of you.' She's a black girl. It's outrageous, because nobody ever says that. You're not supposed to notice any more, are you? So I thought, that's a very daring thing to have to say. And I did say it.

I hadn't heard of *Skins* before I was asked to do it. I read the script quickly on my computer and said 'yes' immediately. Wonderful script. Wonderful dialogue. I thought, 'This is a character who could actually exist and these people say smashing things to each other.' I didn't have to think, 'How am I going to make this sound real?' It was so nicely put together.

It was filmed in Bristol. I was there three days, so we got a lot in. When I got back, I told a friend how much I'd adored doing it and he asked, 'Any chance of your character going on in other episodes?'

I said, 'I really don't think so because she died at the end.'

A few days after the broadcast I received a handwritten letter from Peter Wyngarde, an old friend. He said, 'Adored your flirtatious granny. It explained your grandson's attempts at homosexuality. He obviously adored you! Of course you must come back, as a ghost all eau de nil like Charles's wife in *Blithe Spirit*, giving advice to your grandson'.

Everybody connected with *Skins* was young. Not just the cast – the director was young and the two producers were young. They were so happy about it all; they were thrilled – not about me particularly, but about it. They told me all about its history and how it had built up this amazing fan base and how they had sold it to eighty different countries. The boy who was the lead in the episode I was in was still at school. Oh, it was so lovely to be involved in. To be working with all these very young people.

I suppose it made realise just how long I've been doing this, but not in a bad way; happy for what I've done, but knowing that I'm here now. Somewhere else.

13

Drink, Drugs and Psychiatry

This is a chapter about drink, drugs and psychiatry. Thankfully, based on my own experience and that of the people I've known best, it is very short.

When I first started going out properly with grown-ups everybody would have a drink, and then so would I. The first time I went to a May Ball in Cambridge with my then-boyfriend Tony Shaffer (who'd been at university there), I took it for granted that I could have a little something to drink because everybody else was. To my absolute horror I found that I was actually drunk. Tony was terribly annoyed. He wanted me to have a drink but he didn't want me to be drunk.

Because I would get drunk immediately with very little, it did lead to one or two scrapes, usually connected with falling into bed with people. In the end I just had to say, 'Quite clearly I can't drink, so just give me ginger beer or something.' People who really drink can't bear it when other people don't. They're partly irritated because they think that you're using terrific willpower and they can't, or else they feel that you're bound to be critical of them and they don't like feeling criticised.

Sandy Wilson, who liked a drink, got exasperated with me one time when I went to stay with him in his house in the country. He said, 'I'm going to give you something that you'll be able to drink.' So I waited with interest. It turned out to be Angostura Bitters mixed with tonic and lime. I did start to get a little bit tiddly. He said, 'I can't tell you how little alcohol there is in it.' I still felt it, but not too much, and I liked the taste of it. (I've got some in my kitchen now.)

After I heard about Angostura Bitters, the falling into bed never happened again. If I wanted to fall into bed that's another matter, but it wasn't because I was drunk. Chaps don't like it if you fall into bed only because you're drunk. They like it because you wanted to. So, from every point of view it became better to know how to regulate it.

But, you know, boys can take advantage if you have so much as a cup of tea, perhaps even if you're just carrying a tray of cups of tea, which led to my first kiss. My mother was having an enormous tea party. I was the daughter of the house so I was carrying large trays of tea poured out into cups and this boy, a very unattractive boy, said, 'Ah! I've got you under my power. Now I'm going to kiss you.' I thought, 'I can't very well drop the tray.' I was probably fourteen; he might have been as old as eighteen. I certainly wouldn't have chosen him. I thought my first kiss would be with one masculine arm surrounding me, pulling me towards him. Instead of which it was holding this tray with all these wobbly cups of tea. It wasn't fair and he knew that and he took advantage. And that was my first kiss. How disappointing!

A big jump in time now . . . It was the early 1960s and I was doing a television show. The producer asked, 'Have you got somebody who helps you with your throat?'

I replied, 'Yes, why?'

He said, 'Well, we can't hear you.'

Normally I never had any problem being heard. Clarity is always the thing you aim for, but not being heard . . . it's unheard of!

I phoned my voice man, Ivor Griffiths. He contacted his locum, Ted, and sent him to me at the television studio. He put the mirror down my throat and said, 'Ah, yes.' Then he started to paint my vocal chords with something. Suddenly I became very vivacious.

'I don't understand,' he said. 'I gave you so little.'

I asked, 'Well, what did you give me?'

He said, 'It's the tiniest grain of cocaine. There's almost nothing there.'

Anyway it was very enjoyable because I had become so vivacious; I was telling terribly funny stories and everybody in the rehearsal room was shrieking with laughter.

Ewan Philips told me about LSD when I was living with him in Clarges Street. He said when you took it you could see things that you wouldn't otherwise see, so it was a mind-expanding drug. I didn't take any myself, but I did take half a Purple Heart when we did the first run through of *Valmouth*. At the end of it, Vida Hope, who had never been sure about me in the role, said, 'If you do it like that on the night you'll steal the show.' I didn't take a Purple Heart again, but it did the trick; gave me that extra bit of confidence when I needed it, without me becoming reliant upon it.

Later, I had pot a few times. This would have been the 1970s.

Top: Fenella with James Robertson Justice and Leslie Phillips in *Doctor In Clover* (1966).

Left: Fenella with Tony Curtis in *Drop Dead Darling/ Arrivederci, Baby* (1966).

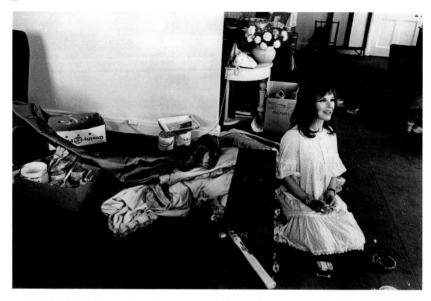

Top: Fenella at her new flat in Connaught Place (1966). Five rooms near Marble Arch, £13 a week! *Bottom left:* Flyer for *So Much To Remember* (1963). A show written by Johnny Whyte and Fenella, inspired by old theatre biographies of actors who didn't waste time on modesty. *Bottom right:* Publicity still for a BBC play, mid-1960s.

Top: Fenella as Valeria Watt in *Carry On Screaming* (1966).
Bottom: Fenella with Kenneth Williams in *Carry On Screaming* (1966).

Fenella with Boots, the theatre cat, at Oxford Playhouse (1972).

Top: Fenella starring in
Colette (1971), Oxford
Playhouse.

*Left: The Fenella Fielding
Show*, Watford (1976). One
of the first ever one-woman
shows. Fenella pictured with
Bernard Lloyd and Mark
Wing-Davey.

Bottom: Portrait session at
Scaioni's Studios.

Top: Fenella on *Channel 5 News* in 2016, when a new run of *Carry On* films was announced. *Bottom:* Fenella with Dame Cleo Laine (2013). Taken in Cleo's kitchen.

Above: Fenella in Portmeirion (2017), to commemorate fifty years since the first broadcast of *The Prisoner*, recreates her Tannoy announcer role. In attendance, Catherine McGoohan, daughter of Patrick McGoohan, was very moved and said her father considered Fenella's role in the series to be 'absolutely integral'.

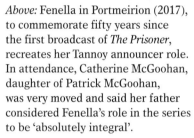

Top right: Fenella at London City Hall (2014). *Centre right:* Connaught Place (2015): 'I used to grow herbs on my balcony. Right there.' *Bottom: Carry On* Group at Westminster Film Fair (2013). Standing, left to right: Shirley Eaton, Patricia Franklin, Liz Fraser, Valerie Leon, Amanda Barrie, Hugh Futcher. Seated, left to right: Jacki Piper, Robin Askwith, Angela Douglas, Fenella Fielding, Anna Karen, Anita Harris, Angela Grant.

Top: Fenella with Simon Russell Beale (2012), performing Greek translations at the Reform Club. *Bottom left:* Fenella Fielding enjoys the sun during a photo shoot for the *Soho Journal. Bottom right:* Fenella Fielding and Simon McKay.

Once, I remember buying a big chunk of it from a woman in my dance class at Covent Garden. She's still in class now. I just sort of stopped so I haven't asked her again. Good to know she's there just in case, though.

In 1963, while I was doing *So Much To Remember* at The Establishment, it wasn't the experience of growing up with my parents that caused me to see a psychiatrist but the naggings of a frustrated boyfriend. He was quite a well-known novelist, Brian. He couldn't understand why I wasn't madly in love with him, which I thought was ridiculous. I was dating him a bit but he wasn't my type and I didn't really want to be obliged to have an affair with him. It's always nice if somebody fancies you, but you don't just want that to be on their side, do you? I thought, 'I don't want to go into detail with you about why I'm not in love with you. The mere fact that I'm not in love with you ought to be sufficient.'

Anyway, he said, 'I'd like you to see my psychiatrist.' I thought, 'See his psychiatrist? It's so ridiculous.' But his psychiatrist, Edward Glover, was at 18 Wimpole Street, which was quite near where I lived, so I went. The psychiatrist asked, 'Name? Age?' Then he asked why I was there. I told him and he said, 'Oh I wouldn't worry about it. I would just go on the way you feel.' It sounded as if this happened with many people, and more often than not. Of course, if Brian had had any sense he'd have just got me drunk. Much cheaper, too, as he paid for me to see the psychiatrist!

14

Famous People: An Aside

This chapter is a short aside about some interesting people I've worked with. A selection of side portions.

I did tons of stuff with Tommy Cooper. He was so lovely. And he had this extraordinary man who'd been a clarinet player or something, called Miff Ferry. He was his agent and he would keep an eye on the script. He would say, 'This isn't right for Tommy. This isn't Tommy's image.' In one of the sketches I did with Tommy, I had to sit on his knee. I was his secretary in it, shorthand typist or something. And he said, 'We're going to have to cut that. Can't sit on his knee.'

I said, 'But that's the point of the lines.'

'Well, you have to say the lines, then, but you don't sit on his knee.'

'They won't make sense.'

'Sorry. It's not Tommy's image.'

Years later, I did something else with Tommy and the same thing happened to Alfie Bass, who was a very well-known actor. Miff changed the whole plot because it didn't fit with Tommy's image. And it spoiled the whole point of that programme.

I know what he meant about Tommy's image, he didn't have sexy remarks, but Tommy wasn't narrow in any other way. He was just amazing. I'll never know why he was so funny, but he was.

These next pieces are so small, they're more like dabs of relish than a side portion, really.

I was on a game show. We were all on the screen in squares – in fact, it was called Celebrity Squares. Groucho Marx was on it. How the game worked, I can't remember; it was a terrible game. But I remember, afterwards, people were trying to impress Groucho with how well they knew his work by doing impressions of him to him, thinking he would be so amused. However, a) they didn't know the material b) they couldn't do it, and c) he didn't give a fuck.

In the early 1960s, I was at the London Palladium to do *Night of a Hundred Stars*. Lots of people were in it – that was the point of it. Millicent Martin was one of them. I walked into the rehearsal and she was on the stage with a hula hoop – I'd never seen one before. And she was doing it as though she'd been doing it all of her life. No wonder she became such a star!

I was in *Hotel Paradiso* in 1999. It was with Rik Mayall and Adrian Edmondson. Bill Nighy was in it too. I remember sitting with Bill on the set of a café, we chatted and he was running himself down in a very funny way. He said, 'Oh well, this is what I've come to. No more romantic leads for me.' And he just made me laugh. Lovely man.

I met Margaret Thatcher when she was prime minister. I didn't like the woman. I'm more of a socialist anyway, but I appreciate it can't work if only fifty per cent of the people support it. I didn't ever want to align myself with politics so my brother, Bas, was upset that I wouldn't appear for him when he was first up for election. He got elected without my help and became big in the Conservative Party. So it was through him that I met Mrs Thatcher, at an event he hosted in the House of Lords.

Apart from anything else I didn't want to let my brother down by looking dim-witted, but I also didn't want to talk politics with her. And I doubted she'd want to talk politics with me. It was a lunch, a social occasion. On the other hand, I was the sister of the host and I ought to speak to his honoured guest, so I said to her – and I meant it very much – that I thought what she had on was wonderful. I said, 'You're so busy. Where do you manage to find such wonderful things to wear?' And to my absolute amazement (well, there is this kind of thing between women, isn't there?) she told me immediately how she'd met these people in America and they made all her things. They knew her measurements and she wore everything they made for her. Always the right colour, the right style, the right thing for the occasion.

She turned to my niece's little daughter, Philomena, who was about four then. She was wearing that sweet little thing that most of the girls of four wore on occasions: a navy velvet frock with a white lace collar. On the yoke of this dress she wore a rather large (on her) sparkling brooch, shaped like a crown. Margaret Thatcher said, 'What a beautiful brooch you're wearing; that lovely crown. Now what you must do . . . ' – in saying this, she put her hands on my niece's shoulders – 'You must turn towards the light and see how the light makes your brooch sparkle even more.' This child, who is now grown up and brilliant, was a very brilliant child but she was totally mesmerised and very biddable. She did turn towards the light and was absolutely gobsmacked – she really didn't have anything to say. I didn't like Thatcher, but she did have something about her.

This next portion is simply about an unnamed dapper man in a bowler hat . . . There's a moment in every TV production called the 'camera day' and it goes on and on. Particularly when you're doing a play – you get wonderfully tired, and that's when people start talking.

This dapper man started talking and what he told me was this . . . What he liked in sex was a great deal of hitting and slapping and knocking about – a bit mutual. He had a new young wife at that point and it was tricky. His wife, she wasn't sixteen or anything, but probably about to turn twenty. She said to him, 'Why don't we do some of that stuff that's in the books you've got by the bedside?' I'm not sure he ever did it with her. I think she was terribly disappointed.

He'd lent me some Victorian porn that was all about knocking about, which I didn't respond to terribly well. It was very sexy because it was all about sex, but the idea of being knocked about still fills me with absolute horror of the inevitable pain, which I don't find thrilling at all.

I said to him, 'What fascinates me is where you find each other to indulge in these practices. How do you know? Is it just a look in somebody's eye?'

He said, 'I reckon so . . . there are certain signals people will recognise if the other person is in the same vein, and you progress from there.'

He told me that one night at some party, he met a girl and she was definitely on. And she said 'yes', she would come back with him if she dressed up as a school girl and he dressed up as a monk. So they went off to Berman's and got some costumes and went back to his place and had a *whizzing time.* The next morning, the phone rang and it was his agent: 'Big movie, but you have to get on the plane to South Africa *now.* You'll be there for three months shooting, at least. Huge money.' So without delay he packed and went. When he got back, finally, it was about six months later, after lots of retakes. He found that he had got this enormous bill from Berman's because he hadn't had time to return the monk's costume. Well, that was a night of rapture that really cost him.

So that's how to get things out of people . . . get them wonderfully tired first.

15

Technique: Taking the Stage

After I'd finished being in *Pieces of Eight* with Kenneth Williams, I met Vladek Sheybal, the Polish actor. He'd been asked to put on some plays in the Little Theatre in Bromley, and he said he'd love me to be in them. One was a French play by Prosper Mérimée, *To Heaven in a Golden Coach*, and the other two were short plays by Tennessee Williams. At an early rehearsal he told me, 'Darling, I'm only going to say one thing to you. In revue, when you first come on, you've got to present your entire character. The audience has to recognise at once what your character is. But in a play, you've got the whole play to do that.' He was right, because in revue even the costume tells the audience what you are, not just the way you present the lines. I found that very useful.

You do pick things up if people are kind enough to tell you when you need it. They'll say, 'If you did it like such and such, that would make the point', and if you listen it can make a real difference.

The actor Hugh Miller said that if you were in a play and

he wanted you to get your face up he'd say, 'Play that line off the end of your pipe'. It was an old-fashioned expression even then, from a time when men still smoked pipes. What he meant was saying a line so your voice would come out and people could still see your face. If you were being real, you might be mumbling with your head down, but being real is not the thing. It's the appearance of being real; the appearance of truth and reality. That's the craft of it.

You learn things for yourself as you go along too, and pass them on. When I was on tour with some not-very-good show, I was very friendly with the stage director. I was telling him about the time I was in pantomime. What I really couldn't bear was the idea of never talking directly to the character I was supposed to talk to. I'd say, 'Good morrow, Princess,' without looking at the person, because we'd both be looking out towards the audience. I thought, 'I can't stand it, so until somebody stops me I shall start the line on the person and turn it gradually to the front.' And nobody did tell me not to, so I knew it was all right.

In the 1980s I did some teaching at the City Lit. Valerie Colgan, who was head of the Drama department, got hold of me and said, 'Come and do some teaching here.' So I did. I was a bit nervous about it. I spoke to a couple of actor friends and they said, 'You probably know a lot more than you realise. All you have to do is decide which aspect of it you're going to teach. The main thing is to get everybody's names right. That's far more important than if you're any good or not.'

I thought about it. Very often you see people on stage, you hardly notice them. Other people, they walk on stage and they're *there*. So I thought, because I had a very wide experience, I'd be able to show people how not to fade out. So I called my classes 'Taking the Stage', which is an acting term. It's not one I made up, and it doesn't mean thieving the stage. It means being there, inhabiting it.

I chose a lot of short pieces that I thought were very interesting and I said, 'If you've got something you'd like to do, fine, otherwise choose a piece from these and we'll take it from there.' My friends said to me beforehand, 'Don't do anything to do with technique. Because technique, by the young, is despised.' It's crazy to say that. You might just as well say about carpentry, 'All you need is a saw and a piece of wood; you don't really need to know anything more.'

There was a huge section of people at that time who decided that the past didn't exist. The only thing that mattered was now. They didn't want to hear how so and so did this or so and so did that because that wasn't sincere and it wasn't them. But I'll tell you a story about Donald Sinden. He was going to be in a play called *London Assurance*, and he'd never, in his entire wonderful career, done any acting where he'd had to wear period costume, so he decided to go to somebody who really knew what's what. He knew this old actor called Baliol Holloway, whom I mentioned earlier; he was the one I'd met when I did a play on the radio called *The Rivals*. And he was jolly old.

Anyway, Donald took Baliol to the Green Room Club and said, 'Bay, I'm going to do *London Assurance*. It's this old play they've dug up, it's very funny. But I've never done a period play in my life. And I've never lifted my arms up above my waist, except maybe to take a book off a shelf. And also I don't know how to do an aside.' They don't have asides in modern plays, but if you're in a period play – especially a comedy or maybe a melodrama – your character will be talking to somebody, and then want to tell their real thoughts to the audience. So you'll say, 'Good morrow, Sir. I'm very pleased to see you.' And then you'll turn to the audience and say, 'I want to find out something from him that only he can tell me, and no one else must know.' Then you turn back to the other character and keep talking.

Well, after tea and scones Baliol got to his feet and said, 'The whole thing about an aside is that you talk to the person you're talking to, then you turn to a certain part of the audience. The rest of the cast freezes. They don't hear you. They keep still. That's the important part. You say to a certain part of the house, "Such and such and such and such." You turn back. Continue the conversation. The next time you have to say an aside, you turn not to that same part of the house but somewhere else entirely. The reason you talk to different parts of the house is that if you continue to talk to the same part, the people in that part start to get a bit paranoid. It's only for their comfort. Each time you do it, the cast freezes. They stay perfectly still. Everybody comes to life afterwards.'

Donald was awfully pleased to be shown these things and to be told how to do them. God knows, he'd been doing other stuff for long enough and he was a great master in all the fields he had been in, but now he was learning something new. He said, 'The awful thing is, there are actors at the moment, who, from their training and their present experience of, say, ten years, won't know how to act in a play from this period at all. They'll never know because they think the only thing that matters is now and modern-ness. They won't even be able to play in a Noël Coward, certainly not a Sheridan. It's such a pity because it's like a carpenter not knowing how to make a tongue-and-groove.'

Acting is a craft. It only becomes an art when it's fantastically good. You can't manage without craft. Otherwise you'd never be able to do it except when you felt like it, when you didn't have a headache or a beastly cold. You've got to be able to do it when you don't feel like it. Somebody once said, 'Actors are people who can do it when they don't feel like it; amateurs are people who can't do it even when they do,' which is just a nasty remark. It is sort of true, but don't go around saying it.

Donald thought it was a terrible shame that that craftsmanship was going to be lacking in a few years. So when I went to teach, I decided I would teach technique. It might sound idiotic to learn how to sit down without looking at the chair, but it looks so mad if you have to look round and keep moving the chair until you're sitting down. If somebody tells you, 'Just feel for the chair leg with the back of your leg,' then it doesn't interfere with what you're saying. It doesn't tell the audience anything that's irrelevant to what's going on, and it means that every move you make tells them something about what's going on.

So anyway, I got the students to do their stuff and I'd talk about it to each person. They were all Equity members, not beginners. If I did speak about something technical, far from not caring to hear it, they *wanted* to know. And really, the most talented ones, you could see that they would take that information and bang it under their skin and be using it for the rest of their lives.

Sometimes when you're teaching, you notice that somebody will be speaking from a scene and putting a lot of emphasis on many different words, which can't work because then nobody knows what's important in what you're talking about. You've got to hit the keyword, and there's no lucky light that says 'This is a keyword'. You've got to know it yourself, otherwise it doesn't mean anything. I said to this fellow, 'I don't quite know why you're stressing that word in particular.'

He said, 'It seems to be an important word.'

I replied, 'Yes, but what are you actually saying in that line?' I told him that I'd just seen a most wonderful season on TV, a few weeks of Bette Davis films. I've always listened to other people's performances with a double ear – one for what they're saying, and one for how I might do it. I listened to Bette Davis and I thought, she never gets the credit for how clever she is. Because if you listen to the words she's saying, it's rubbish. It's awkwardly written. It doesn't make any sense, but she – now this is what you have to learn – she says what the line is about, not hammering on different words. She acts the meaning of the line, not the literal meaning of every word in it, because they're rubbish. The chap I was teaching said, 'I can't tell you what you've revealed. It's really marvellous.' The thing is you've got to learn how to do that. You're not always given great work to act. Some of it is rubbish, and you've got to make it understandable. Get across the meaning, what the person is trying to say. The fellow went away on air. That felt like quite a valuable thing to pass on.

At one time, drama schools always taught people to speak with 'received pronunciation'. If you had an accent, you had to learn 'received pronunciation' because it would otherwise limit you to only playing parts that had your accent. Nowadays they don't bother. I think they should, because you want to be able to play all sorts of parts, according to your abilities.

A hard lesson is that you can't be a leading actor just because you want to be. You can't have somebody playing Richard II when the moment they walk on there's an empty space there. It's a question of weight; a question of presence. When you come into the room, you slightly change the atmosphere of it, just by being there. It's something you're born with. Albert Finney always was a star, even though he started off playing character parts.

When I hadn't quite 'made it' I went down to Pinewood to see a casting man – Buddy someone. I had a handful of photographs that a newspaper photographer had taken of me wearing different hats. With each hat, I assumed a different personality. I thought they were marvellous; showed how versatile I was. When you're inexperienced, you have all sorts of wrong ideas. I showed him these photos, which weren't like studio glamour shots. He said, 'Yes, they're very nice. But you could only play character parts.' At the time, being very innocent, I thought, 'Well, what's wrong with that?' But of course character parts very rarely are leading parts. That's that. You've got to have the weight. Otherwise, you can hear somebody talking but where are they? If you sat in at an audition and watched from the stalls as different people came on, you'd know immediately. Wouldn't be difficult to tell at all. You'd lean forward.

When *So Much To Remember* transferred to the West End, Billy Chapel, who was directing it, said, 'We're going to have auditions at the Duchess Theatre. Now, you've got to be there.'

I said, 'Oh, I don't like the idea of sitting there in judgement of my colleagues.'

He said, 'No, you've got to be there because you're going to be acting with them.' So I did sit there. I sat there very quietly, sort of in the dark, while he sat properly forward. He was lovely. Lots of people aren't lovely at auditions. But whoever they were, he always gave them time and asked them what they'd been doing. What I found really riveting was how, when somebody comes on, you know straight away if they're not right for the show. And other people, you think they would be right if only they were good.

What was fascinating to me was that the ones who weren't right, it wasn't any lack in them. It was just that they were the wrong shape, too tall, too young or possibly too old. They just weren't right for the show. I thought, 'If only I'd known that long ago. If only we'd all known that.' It wasn't that you were no good, you just weren't right for what they were looking for. But you see, you'd always feel it was a terrible lack in you.

I never found I was fearfully good at auditions. I was always a bit embarrassed. As I mentioned earlier, the first job I ever got from an audition was only because I didn't give a damn whether I got it or not, because I was so cross about the pianist being paid twice. So it just shows you, if you don't give a damn you at least give yourself a chance. You're much more likely to be at your best, even if your best doesn't happen to suit the role. I don't see why one shouldn't include that in good advice. God knows, there's hardly any good advice to be given, but that is the best I know.

16

Feldman versus Fielding

When I was a kidlet, I used to wait at the stage door and make impassioned speeches to Alec Guinness. He never gave me the brush-off, never made me feel foolish. I was mad about the theatre . . . Laurence Olivier, Ralph Richardson, Nicholas Hannen and the new young ones – Margaret Leighton, Joyce Redman. I would come up from Edgware on the tube and queue from 5 a.m. at The New Theatre (now the Noël Coward) for cheap tickets for that night, hopefully in the pit – better than the gallery, closer. I loved it. And so of course, I wanted to be an actress.

My cousin Billie wrote to me recently; she reminded me that when we were children I used to put on plays in the garden. She sent me a photograph of us doing it. She said, 'Fin, you cast it, directed it and you got all the costumes together.' It was called *The Princess and the Woodcutter*. (We got it out of a book.) I played the woodcutter and the girl from number 91 was in it, playing the princess. I know I did another play. I was always up to something.

While I was still at school, I worked for the local paper. It started when I was at this little youth club. I made a wall magazine, and I asked all the others to write things and do drawings. I was the editor. I typed out all their contributions and put it all together in the right way, to look attractive. Then I read in the local Edgware paper that they wanted somebody, so I went along with this huge roll of paper, pulled my arms apart and said, 'This is my work!'

They didn't laugh. They asked, 'Look, can you do shorthand?'

'No.'

'Well, it does matter. We can't send you to do court reports because you might not get it right if you can't do shorthand.'

'But I can type.'

'Could you do some pieces for us? Go and interview local people or write some beauty notes.'

So I did. They didn't pay me much, it was by the line, but it was a big thrill. I was still at school so I interviewed some of the people in my class, and because it was the local paper they printed it.

At school, when I was sixteen-ish, I was summoned to see the headmistress because I was walking around with a prospectus from RADA in my science overall pocket. She was very perturbed. She said, 'But look, Fenella, you've got a brain.'

I said, 'Well, I don't know what will happen.'

She asked me, 'Why do you want to do it? Leatrice Jacobs was awfully good in our last play. She's terribly talented and she's not going on stage.' Well, that really hurt.

I left school at sixteen and went straight to art school. I had an idea that I wanted to do fashion drawing. I'd heard of Saint Martin's School of Art, so I thought it must be a very good place and I should go there. Daddy spoke to this Burmese man who lived opposite us, who was an artist. Daddy was very worried that if I went to art school I might see naked men in life class . . . or naked women! He thought it was bound to lead to some sort of licentiousness. He asked this man and he was assured it would be perfectly all right – that his daughter would be safe – so I was allowed to go there. I can't remember it costing anything. Anyway, it was lovely, but I had to do a year's general art before I could specialise, so I did. That's what they wanted, fine. It would be fabulous. But after a while Daddy began to get very restless.

He said, 'I don't think you're going to go on with this.'

'What do you mean?' I asked.

'Oh, if you were really serious about this you'd be running around to manufacturers with ideas and drawings and you're not doing that at all. So what are you doing?'

'Look Daddy, you did know this. They require you to do a year's general art. While I'm doing that I can't be doing the other because I wouldn't be any good.'

'Oh well. Can't see this lasting.'

In the end, before I'd even finished the first year at St Martins he made me leave and that was that. It was hard to be anything that I might want to be because of Daddy. I was always doing things and not finishing them. Like RADA, which is what I did next (and spoke about earlier on).

When I came out of drama school my parents made me go to Pitman's, the business school. It was soul-destroying. I'd never have said at the time, but I was very depressed. I thought I must have been getting a bit above myself thinking I could do this, that or the other, when really all I was good for was to maybe do some shorthand and typing. It wasn't that I despised that; it just wasn't what I wanted.

Daddy was always eager for me to go to work. So he dragged me out of Pitman's before I'd finished, and that made me less competent than I would have been. But he insisted, just like he had about the art school. And because I didn't finish Pitman's that made me semi-equipped. It was so depressing to think I wasn't even a competent shorthand typist.

Anyway, I got jobs in temporary places. The most thrilling job I had was working for a theatrical agent – Al Parker, whom I mentioned earlier on. That was so exciting. He had such incredible people on his books. I had to go and do the switchboard when the switchboard girl was on lunch. All these amazing people with thrilling voices would come on the phone and ask to speak to Al Parker. So I loved that, but at the same time I wasn't brilliant at my actual work, which was shorthand and typing.

I was terrified of Al. I didn't actually work for him, I worked for his beautiful red-haired assistant Josephine. There was one day, she said, 'Al wants you to go in and take down a cable.' So I went in and he said he was going to cable somebody. I said, 'OK, fine. I'll do that.' And I left the room without him ever giving me the message. I was so nervous that I just said, 'Oh yes, I'll send a cable.' Well, how . . . I didn't know. I think that's when they finally decided I wasn't quite suitable for the job. Otherwise it was these ghastly temporary jobs where you'd work for these ghastly men; always at you, you know.

Sort of lecherous.

I did a beauty course afterwards, which I adored and was very good at. There were only a few of us, so we got straight to it. There was even a doctor who came in and taught us physiology, which was very useful if you were going to do massage – face, arms, necks, backs and all that. It was marvellous because I was good at it and I could see it was not a frivolous thing. For example, one of the girls on the course had awful skin, terrible awful red things that came out on her face the whole time. And we had to practice on each other, massage each other's faces. By the end of the course, which I think was only six weeks, her skin was completely clear. So you knew you weren't doing something that was phoney.

After that, when we qualified, they gave us each a huge box of the stuff that they manufactured – not Elizabeth Arden, so not glamorous, but something that was known. So I had this huge case of stuff that was very heavy and I used to go around with it. I advertised in the local paper that I did facials and body massage in the comfort and privacy of your own home. You can imagine the answers that I got – lots of chaps! One burst into tears the moment he said 'Hello'. I think he really thought it was something saucy, and he burst into tears because of his own shame over his desire for sex in this peculiar way.

Anyway, my parents nearly went potty (I was living at home) so I had to cope with all that, but I found some clients and gave them beauty treatments. When I decided to go on the stage regardless, I still did some of this private work, otherwise I couldn't have managed. I didn't earn very much, though. Some of the women that answered my ad lived quite a long way away and I had this heavy bag of equipment . . . it never occurred to me that I didn't need all that muck. Often, to get there in time without my arm falling off, I had to take taxis. So whatever I earned, I'd already spent. Eventually, though, I found a couple of clients who lived near me. Little did they know, but they virtually supported me while I was doing all these terribly underpaid acting jobs.

It's extraordinary . . . years later, I was doing a grapes diet so I went into Harrods, to the grapes department, and I got all these endless bunches of grapes. I was just about to pay, the money was in my hand, when suddenly a woman appeared next to the man sitting at the cash desk and she said, 'Hello.' And I looked at her and I wondered who she was. She looked like a woman who had been terribly ill. Her face was ravaged. She had long hair, but a lot of it was grey. It was blonded, but it didn't look good. And I didn't know who she was.

She said, 'Hello, don't you remember me?'

I didn't want to say, 'No, I don't,' because by this time I was acting and I'd got used to not knowing people who came up to me, and I didn't want to offend her. I was standing there, frozen in time, waiting to pay. The cashier was waiting for me to pay. Everyone was waiting for me to pay. The whole of the grapes department was focused on me. It was incredible.

'Go on,' she said. 'You remember me . . . I'll make you old. I'm the same age as you are.' I still didn't recognise her. And then suddenly a memory came up from nowhere and I said, 'Tell me, did you have a mother whose skin was so marvellous that she could go to bed with all her make-up still on and it didn't make any difference, it didn't hurt her skin, she looked wonderful regardless? Of course I remember you. You haven't changed a bit.' I used to do facials for her and her mother.

Because of Daddy, it was hard to be anything that I might want to be. If I'd done what *he* wanted, I'd never have gone on the stage and I'd still be called Feldman. When I did finally go on the stage, that's when I changed my name. People always did, I thought. Fielding is a translation of Feldman, and I thought it sounded crisper, better . . . and it was a new start. I took seven years off my age, too, so that I could be the age people usually are when they start out and not have to explain anything. Oh, and I learnt to smoke . . . That took me more than a year, but I'd seen lots of films and it seemed to me that it was what actresses did. Now I was an actress, that's what I would have to do! I would smoke.

17

Kenneth Williams

I suppose I'll have to talk about Kenneth Williams some time. I'd done *Valmouth*, which Michael Codron had produced, and Kenneth had done revues that Michael Codron had produced. Codron was going to produce another revue for Kenneth and he very much wanted me to be in it, too. It was *Pieces of Eight*. The material was mainly by Peter Cook, who was a sort of genius really. And he was, without being gay, sort of madly in love with Kenneth. He gave Kenneth some wonderful material. Harold Pinter also contributed material – he really did create a new style of very extraordinary plays. Some of them were very popular and some of them people couldn't bear, but they were always interesting.

Pieces of Eight had a choreographer as the director, which was very good because you get a wonderful balance of things from people who are used to putting on dance shows with climaxes. But although it was an extraordinary show I wasn't that keen because I wanted to get away from the exaggeration of revue; it did make people think you could never pull yourself in to do a quiet play, that you would go over the top – a question of style. I also thought I'd like to see the material first because in a revue that's almost the only thing that matters. Doesn't matter how good you are, if you haven't got material that's good for you, you might as well go and sing in the street.

They said, 'We've got all these writers. We've got Peter Cook, we've got Harold Pinter . . .' My agents were very keen for me to do it. They said, 'You're very lucky to be offered a co-starring role in the West End so soon after you were there with *Valmouth*; it's good to have a follow-up so quickly.'

'Yes', I said, 'but I wish it were a play.'

'Yes, but there isn't one,' they told me. (I'd actually been offered a play by Henry Sherek, who was potty about me, but I didn't like the play very much. I don't think he put it on in the end.)

Everybody was persuading me, saying I would be such a silly girl not to do it, and that I should clinch what I'd been doing. I asked, 'Will I get co-star billing?'

'Yes, yes,' they said. I didn't know until I read a book about Kenneth recently, in which I figured, that he was very angry about not having sole star billing. (If you have co-star billing it means you're equal.) I thought that if I had co-star billing, I'd have co-star rights.

They gave me loads of stuff to look at . . . most of it was rubbish. Most plays are bad; most revue material is bad. Very few people can write wonderful stuff. You'll get drowned in rubbish, but there were various things there that I really did like, and I thought, 'Yes, I can do them with Kenneth.' When we actually started rehearsing, I asked the director, Paddy

Stone, 'What about this sketch? When are we going to start rehearsing this one?'

He said, 'Oh no, darling, we're not doing that.'

'But it was sent to me.'

'No,' he said. 'Kenneth doesn't like it.' And every bloody thing that I thought I would like, Kenneth had said no to, but I hadn't been told. So it was not a happy thing, really. Anyway, in spite of the material not being my special sort of stuff, I still did it very well.

We opened in Liverpool. One morning Kenneth and I came out of the stage door of the theatre into a square. I was wearing black trousers and a black knitted silky jacket with large silver buttons and my hair in a black turban. I think that this was considered rather outré . . . quite curious for then, for there. So I looked a bit unusual . . . And Kenneth just was unusual, his face and his body. There was a group of boys about eighteen years old, they were hobbledehoys. They looked as if they wanted trouble and they made it. They could see he was posh and they could see that I was posh – and I was a bit extreme for that place, for that time in the morning. So they threw stones at Kenneth. He wasn't delighted. We just walked off. Things were sort of OK between us at that time, but this probably didn't help. Although the shows did go terribly well.

When we were out of town with the show, before we came into the West End – at Brighton in particular – I got the most wonderful notices. I'd been there not long before with *Valmouth*, so I thought that the good notices I got in Brighton were on account of that, but he was furious. I wouldn't have thought anybody could be so open about it as to say the things he said to me. We were about to open in the West End, and he came in and quoted these ridiculous notices at me. Things like 'A beautiful butterfly of comedy' and all this. He said, 'It's outrageous.' Then he threatened me. I can't remember exactly what he said, but what he meant was *if I didn't watch out*, if I came it too strong . . . He was threatening me not to be too successful and not to, inexplicably, get these incredible notices when we opened in the West End. I mean, it was awful, I've never been so frightened in all my life. I wish I'd said something about it to Michael Codron.

Kenneth didn't really have to worry. I got bronchitis so I didn't have my voice in full. But it was horrible. He said to me when we were rehearsing, 'You do realise, don't you, that what we've got is rubbish?'

I said, 'Oh?' because I thought it was rather good by then.

He said, 'No, it's absolute rubbish and we're the ones who have to go out there and make fools of ourselves if it's not any good. So you've got to be prepared to ad lib and we'll bring our own selves to it. Can you ad lib?'

I thought, 'I don't know. I never have. I've only ever just done the script. I've never said as much as "good evening" unless somebody wrote it for me.' But when we actually got down to rehearsing it, I found that to my surprise I could. He was quite surprised, too. We turned the two particular sketches we had together into something quite amazing.

After we opened, people used to come and see the show over and over again just to hear what we were saying that particular night, whether we'd changed it at all and gone even further. And then they'd come back a few days later. In the end, Michael Codron began to get cross with us and he said, 'You're going far too far. You're putting in so much stuff you're making the show overrun. Be a little more controlled.' The fact was we did make the sketches very funny. Sometimes I would come out with something good and he thought it was divine. The next night, of course, he would come out with it first – pinch it – or he wouldn't give me the cue, so I couldn't use it.

Then Kenneth had some filming to do, so the mid-week matinée was changed to a late Friday matinée. We did 5 p.m and 8.30 p.m, Fridays and Saturdays included. I can't tell you how exhausting that was. On the days he'd been filming, he really couldn't be bothered with the show. When he was doing our sketches – mine was a sort of supporting part that I'd managed to make into an equal part – he would do so little that I had to make my part carry the sketch, which was exhausting. I managed to do it, but it was hell. For the second show, when he felt a bit more like it, we'd go back to him shouting me down, keeping my stuff out of it. And it was really horrible. It was torture. Sometimes the shouting would happen on nights when there wasn't a matinée. It would happen whenever he felt like it. He'd get his strength up and then *wallop* me for the second show. It was awful.

In the end, we had one particular sketch that was terribly funny. What we were – it sounds so ridiculous – we were two spies who happened to meet in a hotel room. He was dressed in a hat and cape and I was dressed from head to foot in black sequins, very sinuous and shimmery. We'd never met each other before, and we were discussing who had the best spying equipment. We both had a suitcase, and we each had something that if we were caught we could take to poison ourselves. We were vying with each other: who had the best guns, the best microscopes, everything, and the best poison of course – the best death remedy. So in the end we each took it to show that we had the best poison. We were staggering around and not dying and each taking a little bit more. He staggered about; I staggered about. The audience were shrieking. But on this particular night, it went on and on. He was supposed to finally die first and fall on the floor, and then I would take the punch line. Then there would be a blackout, and I would slide offstage, do a quick change and we'd come back on the stage for the finale. On this particular night he wouldn't stop competing with me. I went on and on and he wouldn't keel over. At first I tried to become more extravagant in my movements, but it was no good. So I stopped suddenly and said, 'Last one dead's a sissy.'

The audience shrieked. I then died and went off. When I came back on stage he was looking straight at me. He was white. He came off after the finale and said to anybody who would listen, 'She called me a homosexual in front of the whole audience.' You see, he'd chosen to take it the wrong way. All hell broke loose. He wouldn't speak to me. It was really foul.

I was doing a film at the time, *Foxhole In Cairo*, and as I said before we all had a stomach bug so that was pretty bad in itself, and I was crying my eyes out all the time because Kenneth was so horrible. In the end I said, 'I'd better leave.'

So I asked Michael Codron if he would release me. He didn't want me to go, but I said that I couldn't go on the way things were. I couldn't bear it in my life, this terrible turn. But I did stay on, and things started being OK again, although Kenneth insisted on believing that I'd hurt him. He did awful things to me anyway, even before all this happened.

One day I was in early, in my dressing-room – it was a matinée day, I suppose. I suddenly heard two voices outside. (My dressing-room was below ground with a tiny bit of window.) They were saying how the whole show was Kenneth, really, and that I was so terrible in it. I thought, 'They've seen me come in; they know I'm here and they mean me to hear it.' It went on for about twenty minutes. It was *awful*. Then there was suddenly silence.

Some while later I was talking to someone and I suddenly heard *that* voice. This somebody now wanted to become friends with me, but it was him. It was his voice. I was pretty sure he'd done it to oblige Kenneth. Really, I wish I hadn't said the sissy thing because, even now, there are people who think I said that on stage to 'out' Kenneth publicly when I only said it to bring the sketch to an end. What I said, it's the kind of thing children would say. But Kenneth must have known that all of the audience knew he was gay. He used to make jokes about it on stage.

I did *Carry On Screaming* with him a few years later and we got on fine. I'd forgiven him; I'd put it into the past and I assume that's what he'd done, too. We used to sit and gossip between shots. He had his own little ways, and tons of energy. As soon as he felt that ebbing away he would go off to his room and have a sleep – very much like his character in *Carry On Screaming*! I was asked recently at a Q&A, 'What was it like working with him?'

And I said, 'Well, it's like that nursery rhyme.

> *There was a little girl*
> *Who had a little curl*
> *Right in the middle of her forehead.*
> *When she was good she was very, very good*
> *But when she was bad she was horrid.'*

18

Carry On Screaming

I'm always surprised by the amount of energy and love that *Carry On* fans invest in their adoration of the films. Particularly, I'm always amazed that I'm singled out, because I only did two films.

Carry On Regardless, my first, is just episodes and I'm only in one of them. I seduce Kenneth Connor's character to make my husband jealous and it's all a bit much for Kenneth, especially when my husband catches us. The other one was a leading part. This one seems to have a glow that never leaves it. People just love it . . . *Carry On Screaming*.

Every now and again, five-year-olds who've seen me in it come up to me in the street and say, 'Do you mind if I smoke?' Then they run away. Sometimes they're a lot older than five and they still run away.

Carry On Screaming only took six weeks to shoot. My part of it only took three weeks. I decided it would be funniest if I played it completely straight and, except for the timing, I wouldn't go out of my way to be funny. I was meant to look like that girl who was in *The Addams Family* – Morticia. My whole look was exactly 'Morticia'. I know I was meant to be alluring, but I didn't do it in a clichéd way. I played it as if it was quite ordinary and normal to be wearing a long, low-cut red velvet dress from dawn till dusk.

There's a bit where I'm talking to the butler and then you see a close-up of his toes curling. I'm not doing anything in particular and I played that very straight, too. I wasn't doing any great husky-voiced stuff, so maybe the dress was doing all the work.

I do have these rather mixed feelings towards the hairy monsters. Rather maternal, but also thinking, 'They're terribly attractive.'

The relationships were interesting. The scenes I had with Kenneth Williams . . . I was very direct with him, all the time. I was no-nonsense, the way you might speak to a younger brother. And in it, of course, he was my brother. The bit I liked doing best was with Harry H. Corbett, when he had one of the monster's ears in his hankie.

I say, 'This ear?'

He replies, 'Yes, that there.' It was pure Vaudeville and I adored that.

A while ago, it was the fiftieth anniversary of the *Carry Ons*. Carolyn Quinn (she's often on the radio, does the news a lot) interviewed me, and she asked about the 'smoking' scene. She asked, 'Did you ever think of saying that you couldn't do that scene?'

I replied, 'No, I don't think I did. Why would I say that?' She had the script and read some of it to me. I wanted to say, 'It never sounded like that when *I* did it. You've made me blush.'

It was extraordinary. She wasn't an actress, but somehow in reading it to me she'd gotten across all the stuff that I'd just ridden over because it didn't mean anything to me at the time. I'd had no idea what some of the language meant. I wasn't used to some of it . . . about his whistle and so forth. I think I would have felt very uncomfortable if I had known. I might have asked for some changes, but at the time some of the *double entendres* were just not in my vocabulary. And that's a fact.

I was in some difficulty in that scene because the dress had been altered and not put back as it had been. I couldn't bend or move around in it any more. They'd done a wardrobe test on the dress and then they'd thought that they'd like to try cutting out a diamond shape on the stomach and filling it in with black fishnet. Well, they did a wardrobe test on that and thought, 'No, it's too distracting. Every time you breathe that mesh moves.' That would be flesh, mesh and everything, all moving at the same time. They put the piece back in, but there wasn't anything extra so it raised the waist and was much tighter around the diaphragm than it had been. I couldn't sit down – although I wasn't supposed to sit down in it anyway, or it would get out of shape. So they gave me a leaning board. It's at an angle, and you lean against it so you can take the weight off your feet without creasing your frock. That's really what it's for. It was very uncomfortable, but I could undo the zip at the back and only do it up when I was ready to go again.

In the 'smoking' scene, we had to work out where I could sit balanced without rocking back and forth. It was all really quite hard to do in that dress because my movement was so limited; the velvet dress stuck to the sofa, so it was never easy to do the reclining. I had this awful feeling of responsibility to the wardrobe to not reduce the dress to a rag until the shooting was over. They had such a tight budget for costumes that I'm surprised they didn't ask me to make the dress myself. I even had to pay for my own ring! The wardrobe mistress took me to Paris House, a costume jewellery shop in South Molton Street, and she said, 'Well darling, I want you to have the cube earrings. You can buy the ring if you want, but you'll have to pay for it yourself.' So I did. I paid nine quid. That was quite a lot for a piece of rubbish in 1966. I've still got it, though.

As I said before, they never did retakes in *Carry On* . . . only if the set fell in or if somebody completely forgot their lines. The director, Gerry Thomas, had got his editing in mind before he actually filmed it. That's why he could be so quick, and everyone was used to it. Do a scene. Finish. Do a scene. Finish. But after we'd done the first take of the 'smoking' scene I said to Gerry that I didn't think Harry was coming on to me enough and could we please do it again. So we *did* do it again, but Harry didn't do it any differently . . . so I just went on with it. Emboldened by my great coup of getting a retake, after another scene I asked, 'Darling, do you think we could do that bit again?'

'Oh no, you've had your retake,' Gerry replied.

As for what they paid me for being in the film . . . I've never queried what I've been paid for any of the films I did. I took it for granted that my agents would take care of that because I was busy doing other things simultaneously, as a lot of us were. But I was shattered later to find out how much the people who did get good money actually got. Really amazed. I read that I got £300 a week, and there's nothing for TV showings now or DVD sales.

Still, it's amazing to be remembered for the *Carry Ons* because nobody thought *Carry on Screaming* or any of them would last. Everybody was very sniffy about all of them. Yet while we were filming we went to the rushes every day and laughed like anything seeing other people's scenes and vice versa; we thought it was good. I will say, though, that when we all went to the first screening of *Carry On Screaming* we did honestly sit there with faces of stone. Seeing them all stitched together, we thought, 'Oh dear.' It wasn't a première, just a first screening, and we were sitting there among members of the public – if they had fallen about laughing, I expect we would have, but they didn't. It wasn't until a year or so afterwards that I saw it on telly, and thought it was very good.

Carry On Screaming's reviews weren't great when it came out. There was a half-page in the *Observer*, when it was a *broad* broadsheet, enormous. It was written by Penelope Gilliatt, who was very much to the fore at that time. She was an intellectual but she happened to be rather beautiful and was married to a Dr Roger Gilliatt. She was having an affair with John Osborne, whom she later married, and was very brainy. She said what a ghastly film it was, but obviously there was nothing else to review that week because she used a great deal of space. She said, more or less, that the director had 'edited the film like slapping slices of cold ham together'. She also said that everybody gave terrible performances except for me: 'If only they'd all done it like Fenella Fielding everything would have been all right.' It was a lovely notice for me, but it was ghastly to think what the others must have thought. And anyway, it isn't true.

Felix Barker in the *Evening News* said I was obliged to perform a scene of prolonged indecency. He meant the 'smoking' scene. He said he hoped 'that in the future Miss Fielding won't do this kind of thing again.' I thought, 'What? He's mad.' Then I suddenly got it! What he meant . . . the funny thing is, if I had got it at the time; I don't think I could have done the scene so well.

I turned down a few *Carry On* roles. I was offered Cleopatra in *Carry On Cleo*, but it clashed with my schedule. That would have been a nice thing to do. *Carry On Cabby* I just didn't like the sound of, though. All the cab drivers were girls with immense boobs; I don't know if they turned out to have them in the film, but in the script they did. And I thought, how disgusting, because they didn't seem to have anything else about them. So I thought it was rather offensive. There were some other ones that, after reading the script, my agent more or less turned down for me. *Carry On Camping* was one; I got the impression it was a bit much. Usually your agent says, 'I don't know, see what you think of it. Read the script and we'll talk about it.' Sometimes they go so far as to tell you, 'It's a wonderful part , you really ought to do it.'

My darling then-agent, Peter Crouch, had the most wonderful way of turning things down. People never took offence. He would say, 'I've spoken to her and she's not drawn to the role.' When I first went to Peter Crouch, I said, 'I'm just sick of being looked at in that particular way, for the same kind of parts.'

He asked me, 'What do you want to do?'

I said, 'I do want to do some straight plays. I do want to do some Shakespeare and so forth, but I don't want to be laughed out of court.'

He said, 'Fine, but you'll have to be prepared to turn a lot down.' I think despite everything he'd have been jolly glad if I had done *Cleo*, and there didn't seem to be any 'yes or no' about *Screaming*. Nevertheless, he had the right idea. And he sent me to see a particular TV playwright at the BBC, Alan somebody or other. This guy talked to me and said, 'I have to say you're not what I expected.' I was pleased. And he said, 'It's so ridiculous, but I would never had said yes to meeting you if it hadn't been for your particular agent'. Because they trusted him.

My agent would say, 'Yes, yes, I know she was doing things where people were smacking her bottom, but she'd be wonderful as Queen Elizabeth XIX'

And they'd say, 'All right Pete, if you say so.' And they'd often change their minds. Pete was a bit exceptional in that way. He went on being a very good agent, but the only thing that got him in the end was the drink. I had to leave him then.

I remember that once Gerry Thomas – who directed the *Carry Ons* – was doing something, not a film, and he got together a lot of people to talk about comedy. He talked to us one by one in the Orangery at Holland Park (that lovely place where it's all glass like a great conservatory). He stuck me against the glass panels and asked lots of questions; I seem to remember being there about two hours. One of the questions he asked was, 'Can you say if there was anybody who influenced you greatly?' And I thought and thought and thought and I said,

'Oh gosh Gerry, I'm terribly sorry, but I can't really think of anybody who did. I know that when I was a beginner I used to absolutely worship Margaret Leighton, and I expect I absorbed a little of her, but that's not really a great deal to do with comedy, is it?'

Then I told him about Nino The Wonder Dog, who I was so keen on in the 1950s and who I thought was so terribly funny. It was an act at The Palladium, a variety act. This man had lots of dogs who jumped about and sat on things and wagged their tails and lifted one paw and did various tricks, but the big star of it was Nino The Wonder Dog, who I think was a little Jack Russell. He had a terrific personality. (The dog man, I have to say was rather plain, a bit bald in a very unattractive way because it didn't look right on a variety stage to have no make-up and a half-bald head and to wear things like braces with rolled-up shirt sleeves.)

But on came Nino, and he did his stuff and he'd get terrific applause and then he would go right down stage to the front and sit there and look up at the gallery, which is what you must do: dress circle first, gallery, stalls. He'd lift one paw, then he'd rush off and come back again and hesitate at the wings and then rush on to the centre and take another call, smiling like dogs do. They always look as if they are smiling when their tongues are out. And I used to think that if I ever got to the stage where I could come on and just stand there, with the audience riveted before I have to utter a word, then I'd know I'd really got it.

So I told Gerry that, and I can't remember much else really, but I know I said to him afterwards, 'Darling, I'm terribly sorry, I couldn't think of anybody who'd influenced me.' He told me, 'That's all right, practically nobody could. Certainly Joan Sims couldn't think of anybody.' I said, 'That's all right then.'

Then afterwards, to my absolute horror and some fury, I found out that what we were recording wasn't one programme – what he'd done is he'd filmed all these different people and he chopped bits off each one and made about five programmes all out of one afternoon's recording with each person. It saved him an awful lot of money, but we could have all had five fees for being in five programmes. Ooh! So I was very cross with Gerry Thomas for that, but I didn't resent it because he was so lovely.

19

Finale

This is the finale. I've spoken mainly about the 1950s and
1960s, as I've always thought in biographies it's the early
struggles and early successes that make the best read. Well,
of course I've continued working and done lots since. I've
never stopped.

There were all these terrible tours in the 1970s. Going out
of town is very different from shows that are heading into
London, the West End. A whole different shmear. I met some
lovely people, though. *Gigi,* for instance, was not a great
production but I made a marvellous friend in Jean Bayless.
I still see her. You form such lovely alliances and friendships
when you're touring. And sometimes the audience enjoys
the show so much, some of them follow you from town to
town. So it's nice to know they really meant it.

I never stopped taking performing seriously. It's always
been important to me. One morning, in the 1980s, I slept in
and I was home in London when I should have already been
on my way to Chichester for a matinée appearance. It was

too late to take the train and it would have taken forever in a taxi. I thought a helicopter would be the quickest. I looked in the Yellow Pages, and there were three places. I rang them all and found that one of them could do it in time. They picked me up somewhere like Victoria, although I'm not sure about that. It worked: I arrived in time for the show! Some of the cast thought I was mad. They said, 'But the understudy could have gone on.' I wasn't going to let her have a look in!

Over all the years, I've got to do a great many things. There's been lots of music ... I made a record in 1966, *Big Bad Mouse*. Later, I adored doing *The Façade Suite*, which was speaking Edith Sitwell's poetry over music. Loads of performances: one was in 1970 at the Queen Elizabeth Hall. I did that with Michael Flanders and The Nash Ensemble doing the music, Edward Downes conducting – a marvellous conductor. As recently as 2007, I was in Jarvis Cocker's Meltdown Festival. There were lots of people there to do Disney songs. Somewhere between Grace Jones and Pete Doherty, I did *Feed The Birds (Tuppence a Bag)*.

For some roles I've had to develop other skills, besides acting or singing. Like playing the piano on stage for *Let's Get A Divorce*, horse-riding lessons in Hyde Park for *Drop Dead Darling* (although not quite enough lessons – for some shots they used a double in the film). I also learned something from the *Giselle* ballet for *Doctor In Clover*. Although sometimes you don't have to actually do the thing – I once played a ballerina, but I didn't dance ballet. In fact, I must have worn that fabulous *Swan Lake* headdress in at least three different roles without ever getting on point.

Mark Kermode got in touch with me in the mid-nineties. He wanted me to review some films with him, and then we went on the Danny Baker show on Radio 5 to deliver our great words of wisdom. Mark was pretty young and I suppose he was just starting out, but I knew his name. He was lovely. We went to two different films – the one I remember is *French Kiss* with Kevin Kline and Meg Ryan.

Of course, there were lots of things I didn't get to do and people I didn't get to work with. I notice that people who work with Trevor Nunn always have praise for him. I went to see Ian McKellen playing Iago in *Othello* with Willard White, and I said to Ian afterwards, 'I loved the way that in that scene where you get the guy drunk you're only having very little to drink out of a very small glass.' He said, 'Oh, that was Trevor's idea.'

Sadly, I didn't get to work with Trevor. Of course, I've worked with lots of other people who I thought were very good indeed. It's marvellous when you work with somebody and they don't worry whether it's your idea or theirs; it's like that moment when you're on stage with somebody and you put out your hand to find that it's in the other person's hand already.

Looking back at what I've done, it seems I've often been a lady or a tart, but of course there was plenty in between. For one thing, James Hogan and Christopher Reason wrote a couple of plays that we did as a double bill, and I was neither a lady *nor* a tart in either. I've done lots at Chichester Festival, too: *The Beaux' Strategem*, *An Italian Straw Hat*, *Look After Lulu* – even a revival of *Valmouth* in 1982.

I also had a non-singing part, Madam Pfeil, in *Der Schauspieldirektor* [Der Shou-speel-dee-rektor], which means 'The Impressario'. It was an opera at Spitalfields in the late 1990s. They showed me some dialogue that was right for the period, but it was terrible, so I said, 'I've got a friend who could write wonderful scenes for me to do.' And I got in touch with Perry Pontac, a brilliant American – I'd been in one of his plays when he first came over. He wrote some fabulous scenes, really marvellous. They were right in period and terribly funny on top of it.

At the time, Spitalfields was a wonderful thing. A big empty space near the centre of town; if you'd wanted to buy a flat that was the moment. It's well known for the market, which was wonderful then: marvellous second-hand bookshops, paintings and folio graphs. The whole area developed very quickly. The opera house held 500 people. It was obviously temporary; it had this wonderful umbrella-type roof and a raked auditorium. I can't remember how long it was there or how long we did the opera for; probably only two or three weeks.

I used to do poetry recitals at Stratford-upon-Avon with Patrick Garland, too. He'd put together readings of poetry on certain subjects; it would be one actor, one actress. I did quite a lot of those. You do them for virtually nothing, really, but it was such a pleasure. I've done poetry on television, which is what I think led to my being asked to do the recitals at Stratford. It was lovely to be doing those, when people might otherwise think of you as an actress who just larks about.

More people will see you in a film than will ever see you in a stage run, probably. And that is really extraordinary. Millions of people will have seen me in *Carry On Screaming* who won't have seen me in anything else at all, not even other films. And a lot of people know me from *The Prisoner*, just for my voice. I would say over a third of my fan mail comes from that, still. Which is lovely, but at the same time it's such a shame when I think of some of the things I've done.

I'd like to be known for doing the Victorien Sardou play *Let's Get A Divorce* (1966), which I did at the Mermaid. I regard it as the moment when I really got my acting badge (like girl guides get). On the whole I got remarkable reviews that weren't patronising at all, and some people who hadn't liked me before suddenly did like me.

I'd also like to be known for two Ibsen plays I did. One of these was *Hedda*, which I also did on the radio with Ian McKellen and a marvellous cast. I also played Nora in *A Doll's House*. Wonderful part. Some of my fondest friends were unsure, but I said, 'No, I'm going to do it.' I got the most amazing response and it had the most brilliant cast. A particular critic, Jack Tinker, saw me play Nora, and forever afterwards if he saw anybody else do it he always held me to measure against. Whenever I met him he used to fall on his knees. So it couldn't have been that bad, could it?

A few years ago I met a man in the street who had been to quite a few of my shows in the past. It was like he had my whole career in his fist. It made me feel I wasn't imagining it, but the thing about a stage show is it's only remembered in the minds of people who saw it.

Of course, you know I called this book *Do You Mind If I Smoke?* because it was a line in *Carry On Screaming*. People so often say it to me. Even Boy George, when I bumped into him one lunchtime. That's when I decided that was the name for the book.

As I mentioned earlier, when I became an actress and I decided to learn to smoke, it took me a year. But I thought, that's what actresses do, they smoke, so I persevered. Later on, though, I wanted to stop. I once appeared on television on *The Eamonn Andrews Show* with what looked like a cigarette in a holder in my hand. Eamonn tried to light it for me and I stopped him. This was on air. At the break he asked, 'Why didn't you let me light your cigarette?'

I said, 'It's not a real cigarette. It's to help me to give it up.'

He said, 'Well, when we get back on air, you'll have to give an explanation.' So I did, and after that I couldn't buy these substitute cigarettes where I lived. They were completely sold out there, probably everywhere else too. They didn't work, though.

It was much later when I gave up smoking, just in time. It was the late 1970s. I'd tried about four times and had always gone back. Somebody had put me on to an acupuncturist, but for something else. I was broke and living in Earls Court, and I was told about an acupuncturist round there, Robert Graham. He only charged a fiver, apparently. A fiver was about all I could manage.

I went because I was in agony when I lifted my arm beyond a certain point. He asked me, 'Well, why should you want to?'

I said, 'I want to be able to do everything with my arms that I used to do.'

He said, 'What about your other arm?'

I said, 'That's fine.'

He said, 'Well, you're all right then, aren't you?'

I thought, 'It's no wonder you're out here and only charging a fiver. You're absolutely hopeless.' But I said, 'Well, while I'm here, what about my smoking?'

His face lit up. It was obviously the one thing he could do. What he did was he put a little needle into a particular part of my ear. He said, 'This connects with the hypothalamus, which is the centre of all addictive cravings.' And what it was like, this needle, was the backside of an earring – it had a little stopper on the end. He gave me instructions, he said, 'When you feel you can't manage without a cigarette, just press that. Be careful when you're washing your hair, and if it falls out come back and I'll put it back in for you.'

To my absolute amazement, it worked. After four or five days I rang up my chap and told him that I hadn't smoked for four days. He said, 'Well keep on with it, that's wonderful.' After about two weeks, I got a terribly overblown disgust for the smell of cigarettes. If anybody was a smoker, I could smell it on them and couldn't bear it; there was a lot of shifting in my seat. Then that went away, and after that I was clear and didn't need to smoke any more. Isn't that amazing?

I've mentioned a few boyfriends during these chapters. If I met somebody there might be some great affair. Some I lived with, some lived with other people. And also – I don't know that I want to put this in a book, really, but here we go – I had two lovers at once for twenty years. I loved them both. Never committing; never having a marriage that could have gone awful. They didn't know about each other. I went away with them, but not often.

I didn't have children, of course. I don't think I regret that. There's always been so much to do. Being an actress is the thing that's been most important to me. I realised very early on that having a chap wasn't going to be straightforward. The sudden success of *Valmouth* immediately made things much harder in my private life. At that time I had a boyfriend that I'd been wanting to leave for ages; I knew he was hanging on to me. The moment I got this part, he actually said to me, 'You'll have to stay with me now or everyone will think you've dropped me because of this show, that you're too big for your boots.' Weirdly, years later I found an old letter from him and I could feel that whole thing coming over me again . . . the guilt and how manipulative he was.

A bit of success and it gets harder. You can meet people, have supper with them . . . then it all changes. That's when people can see what you're actually like, and that the performance is not the person. What's sitting there with them is the person. And then there's me . . . what I do. One day Sandy Wilson told me I was getting a bit starry-eyed. I listened to him and calmed down.

I did meet somebody a few years ago I really thought I would marry. I knew he loved me, but then he died. Mainly, though, I've always dodged marriage, found a way out of it. There was somebody else before that, way back, who I was going to marry, but he turned out to be an alcoholic. He couldn't stop. It was such a shame. He didn't stop until after I'd broken it off with him, and then three years had passed and it was too late. I'd lost the feeling.

I've avoided saying this until now, but actually I turned down *Carry On Cleo* to go to New York to spend time with an American boy I'd met in London. I was led to think that it was on between us, but when I got there it was all awkward. It was in the winter. I was only there for a few weeks. I was wearing my little fur coat, but it was like wearing a bit of tissue paper. Winter in New York is bitterly cold. I should have done *Cleo,* really.

I think I'm known for my eyelashes. In the 1960s Dusty Springfield was asked about her eye make-up and she said, 'Fenella Fielding's been a very big influence.' The story was syndicated worldwide and the cost for my press cutting service that month was enormous. It was all the same story, sent to me in many envelopes. It cost me a fortune! And then, of course, there is the expense of the actual eyelashes.

One day I got home and went to my dressing-room table in the bathroom, where I'd left a pair of eyelashes in a white ashtray that was shaped like a shell, and my eyelashes were gone. I asked my cleaning lady if she knew anything about it. She told me, 'Oh, I threw them away because they looked like spiders'. Oh God, if she knew how much those spiders cost: they were made by a very famous film make-up man and you could only get them directly from him. They were made of what looked like shaped plastic thread, curved and graduated. They were very long-lasting, but you had to sort of meld them gradually into a shape. They weren't the easiest possible thing, and I'd just got them ready to use and now they were gone. Anyway, that was that. They were spiders as far as she was concerned, and they went the way of all spiders.

Eyelashes that look like spiders – the very idea. But as Tony Warren (who wrote *Coronation Street*) said to me when I was in *Jubilee Girl*, 'Oh yes, darling! If you're going to wear eyelashes, really wear them!' It's not all glamour, though, the eyelashes. I went to see *La La Land* recently and I cried so hard at the end that one fell right off.

I've done lots and lots of voice work over the years, so many adverts in little studios in Soho. Less work now, so when I'm told by somebody that they were asked to record something in a Fenella Fielding voice, I think, 'Bloody cheek. Why didn't they ask me?'

I mentioned that I went for elocution lessons when I was young, lots of people did at that time. Well, I remember finding out that when I was little some mothers used to send their children round to play with me, so that it might rub off on them. But the way I spoke seemed normal to me.

I had an encounter once, on a theatre tour in the late 1990s. It was late morning and I went to a caff in Gainsborough. I had a quick 'discuss' with the woman behind the counter about what to have, and then I ordered half a chip butty. This chap, who was at another table with his friends, leaned forward and said, 'Do you always talk like that?' He wasn't being casual or friendly. I took a deep breath and I said, 'Yes, I suppose I do, because I come from London. Just as you talk the way you do, because of where you're from.' I don't remember him saying much more after that, but it was very frightening. I don't think he would have come over and hit me, but for a moment it felt like it.

I'll be ninety this year, I can't believe it! I'm still working, though. I was in a play on Radio 4 recently called *Between the Lines*. It was lovely to do. And those nice people who do Radio 4 news programmes, Eddie Mair and Paddy O'Connell, sometimes get me to come in and read something for them, like 'Horticultural Filth'.

On stage, I've been doing some gorgeous, very speakable translations of Greek poetry and classics. I've also done some poetry with a Liverpool poet called Gerry Potter. And Simon McKay ... well, we wrote this book together. We go on stage and do Q&A nights. And I've done lots of readings of chapters for this book at the Phoenix Artist Club, just to see how it all went. I guess it went well because we recorded it as an audio book first, and now it's a print book. It took us six years, but I'm delighted to have done it. And I'd like to say thank you for listening, and reading.

Appendix:
Diaries 1958–1968

The following extracts are from Fenella's appointment diaries. They're taken from the busiest and most exciting years of her life; 1958–1968. In essence it's a simple list of what she was doing, but what she was doing week after week was so extraordinary and so hectic that it makes for fascinating reading. Fenella has retrospectively elaborated on some entries to give little anecdotes or comments.

The appointment diaries give a feel of what happens in the lead-up to filming or a stage show – meetings, costume fittings and so on. Reading through Fenella's relentless schedule gives some idea of how incredibly popular and admired she was in these years, constantly on television and radio – any excuse was used to get her on a chat show, it seems. And there's a practically endless list of voiceovers made in little sound rooms in Soho. Yet more evidence of that incredible voice and how much it has been appreciated over the years.

1958

8 January	Voice lesson with Clifford Turner
9 January	Music rehearsal with Stanley Myers
13 January	Perform cabaret at a ball in Wolverhampton with Stanley Myers
16 January	Voiceover *Batchelor's Cigarettes*
17 January	See Carl Hyson (club booking agent)
20 January	See Alan Tarrant (TV director)
22 January	Voiceover *Delucia* (fruit drink) at Olympia
29 January	Voiceover *Delucia* 'Another one. So the first one must have been brilliant!'
30 January	Voiceover *Berlei Bras* at Denmark Street
31 January	Retake for Hughie Green at Regent Studios
2 February	Appear on *Monday Show* for Hughie Green at Wembley Studios
4 February	Rehearsals begin for *Look Back In Anger*
6 February	Voiceover *Knights Castile Soap*
8 February	Attended a casting with Vivien Ellis. 'I said, "But I've got laryngitis." He insisted that I came along. Then he said I wasn't suitable because I didn't sound right. Perhaps he didn't know what laryngitis was.'
10 February	First night of *Look Back in Anger* at Croydon Palace for two weeks
10 February	Appear in Cascade Nightclub floor show (run till 22 February 1958)
11 February	Voiceover *Fenolia Soap*
19 February	Interview with Bill Bourne for a paper called *Showbiz*
25 February	Audition for Dennis Carey's *Juanita*. 'He liked me.'
3 to 6 March	Rehearse *Design For Murder* TV play directed by Michael Elliott (Rehearsals at Cecil Sharp House, last one at Wood Green Empire)
8 March	Appear on *Dickie Valentine Show* from Wood Green Empire (TV broadcast)
10 March	Costume fitting at BBC Lime Grove
14 March	Record for Hughie Green at Studio G, BBC Lime Grove
15 March	From noon prepare for 8 p.m. live transmission of *Design for Murder*
16 March	Rehearse for Hughie Green
17 March	Rehearse for Hughie Green then appear on *Monday Show*
19 March	Costume fitting at Berman's
20 March	Rehearse at Dinely's for police concert
24 March	Voiceover *Cool Tan*
26–30 March	Rehearse for Hughie Green *Monday Show* (Rehearsals at Hilton House although final day was at Prince's Theatre.)
31 March	Transmission of *Monday Show* from Wembley Studios
2 April	Meet Ian Grant (songwriter) to get some new material
14 April	*Monday Show* transmission. 'Most likely sketches with Hughie Green.'

15–17 April	Rehearse *Monday Show*
18 April	Perform *Army Game* (an episode in a series, probably radio)
20 April	Attend debate about censorship at Royal Court
22 April	Meet Marius Goring (actor) at Grosvenor House
25 April	Meet Ronald Eyre (director) at Lime Grove
12 May	Appear on *Tonight* (topical show hosted by Ned Sherrin), Music Room at 3.30 p.m., Lime Grove Studios. 'I probably had a number or some dialogue. It went out live.'
13 May	Rehearse at Film House at 4 p.m. Evening performance of *Chelsea at 8* at The Chelsea Palace (television broadcast)
15 May	Voiceover *Venetian Blinds*
15 May	Perform sketch in show called *Casino de Paris*
24 May	See *The Hamlet of Stepney Green* (Oxford)
25 May	See ETC Revue dress rehearsal (Oxford)
17 June	Appear *Late London* (light entertainment show at 11.30 p.m.), Room 316 at TV House
19 June	Voiceover *Batchelor Soup*. Soho Square
7 July	Interview with Joseph Janni at Pinewood
25 July	Meet Sunny Zal (agent) and Ronnie Wolf (scriptwriter). Nothing came of it.
28 July	Voiceover for ad firm Young & Rubican
29 July	Voiceover *Birds Raspberry Custard* at Star Sound Studio
31 July	Meet Sandy Wilson about *Valmouth*
31 July	Meet Johnny Whyte about some new material
1 August	Audition for director at Cambridge – linked to Johnny Whyte
6 August	Voiceover *Fried Bliss*
9 August	See Red Mitchell about transposing keys for some songs
16 August	*Valmouth* party at Vida Hope's home in 6 Frognal Gardens at 7.30 p.m.
17 August	Rehearsals begin for *Valmouth* at YWCA
15 September	*Valmouth* first night at New Shakespeare in Liverpool (for one week). 'Vida Hope got it down from four-and-a-half hours to two-and-three-quarters'
2 October	*Valmouth* first night at Lyric Hammersmith
8 October	Voiceover for Benson's ad firm
13 October	Voiceover *Omo*
17 October	Voiceover *Murray Caramels*
22 October	Voiceover *Advocaat*
28 October	Meet with people from JC Williamson Theatres at Panton House. 'They wanted me to go to Australia. Lots of people went there and had a lovely time, but I thought I needed to be around in case I was doing something "proper" in London.'

30 October	Voiceover for firm Coleman, Prentice & Varley
11 November	Voiceover *Marmite*
17 November	Meet David Booth Elstree
21 and 24 November	Record part in television show *Glencannon* at Elstree
28 November	Voiceover *Rank Screen Services*
8 December	Voiceover *Knor Suisse* (soup in a cube)
10 December	Voiceover *Handy Andy* (household cleaner) 'This got endless repeats.'
13 December	*Valmouth* closed at Lyric. 'Writer Firbank and Sandy Wilson had a huge following.'
15 December	Voiceover at Pathe House
16 December	Voiceover at Dineley's Studios
17 December	Lunch at Ritz with Sandy Wilson and his boyfriend John
31 December	Meet Kenneth Carten. 'He became my new agent. It was better than where I was and a big step up for me.'

1959

5 January	Rehearse *Valmouth* at Saville Theatre
7 January	Film *Sapphire* at Pinewood (Fenella's first film appearance. Directed by Basil Dearden.)
19 January	First night of *Valmouth* at Brighton Theatre Royal
27 January	First night of *Valmouth* at Saville Theatre for twelve weeks (until 25 April)
29 January	ITN *Late Extra* – piece filmed at Fenella's flat in Eastbourne Mews
30–31 January	Record *Valmouth* LP
4 February	*Time Magazine* photocall
10 February	*Harper's Bazaar* photocall
13 February	*Educating Archie*, Radio 4 comedy with a ventriloquist
1 March	Move out of Eastbourne Mews temporarily to Jane Wenham's flat in Hyde Park Square
5 March	Audition *20th Century Fox*
19 March	Meet Michael Codron at The Ivy re. *Pieces of Eight*
20 March	Rehearse at Playhouse for *That's Life*
25 April	Last night of *Valmouth*
29 April	Walton on Thames Studios, *Four Just Men* for BBC (three days' work)
9 May	See *Sapphire* in the cinema
11 May	Fitting at 10 a.m. for Hackney Empire
11 May	Rehearse for Hughie Green at Cecil Sharp House
12 May	Film at Hackney Empire for Hughie Green

13 May	Rehearse at Cecil Sharp House for Hughie Green
15 May	Camera rehearsal for Hughie Green
16 May	Hughie Green *Saturday Spectacular* at Wood Green Studios
30 June	Voiceover *Berlei Bras*
1 July	Appear on a music programme *Swinging Down The Lane* at TV Centre
2 July	Fitting for *Follow a Star* film (starring Norman Wisdom)
8 July	Voiceover *Berlei Bras*
17 July	Appear in a TV comedy *Brigadier Wellington-Bull* at Lime Grove
20 July	*Tell The Truth* game show run-through at Hackney Empire
21 July	Voiceover *Polo Mints*
22 July	Fitting at Berman's for *Night of a Hundred Stars*
23 July	Appear in *Night of a Hundred Stars*, midnight at the London Palladium
27 July	*Tell The Truth* game show broadcast live
4 August	*Pieces of Eight* rehearsal starts
6 August	*Follow A Star* start filming (probably at Shepperton)
31 August	First night of *Pieces of Eight* in Oxford
7 September	First night of *Pieces of Eight* in Liverpool
14 September	First night of *Pieces of Eight* in Brighton
23 September	First night of *Pieces of Eight* in London Apollo. 'I've found a list of all the people who sent me cards, gifts; first-night telegrams from Michael Codron the producer, Paddy Stone the director, Peter Cook the author, Frank Horrocks the band leader, the stage management and the other seven in the company. And I sent them telegrams.'
24 September	ITN Interview alongside Kenneth Williams
25 September	Photocall for *News of The World*
28–29 September	Record *Pieces of Eight* at Decca for LP
30 September	Saw Lena Horne at Savoy
1 October	Rehearse at Victoria Palace at 12 p.m.
1 October	Interview for *The Stage* magazine
2 October	Record audio *Pieces of Eight* for Gala Records
5 October	Lunch at *Caprice* with Michael Codron
5 October	Record audio *Pieces of Eight* for Gala Records. 'Sandy insisted on using that awful organ on the recording; he loved the sound, but also it was too expensive to have an orchestra.'
10 and 13 October	Fitting for *Danger Man* with Raymond Ray
13 October	Variety Club Luncheon at the Savoy 12.45 p.m. 'First time I've ever been invited, so that's a step up. It's because I'm in a West End show.'
16 October	Fitting for *Danger Man* with Raymond Ray. 'He was ever so good. He used to tear the material, never cut it. It always looked wonderful.'
25 November	Film *Danger Man* at MGM

18 December	Party at The Apollo for 100th show of *Pieces of Eight*
19 December	Move from Jane Wenham's flat in Hyde Park Square to own flat at 15 Hyde Park Square. 'I'd been in Jane's flat longer than she had wanted!'
20 December	Mr Appleton 10.30 a.m. 'He came to cover my chaise longue. I got it from the set of *Jubilee Girl*. At the end of the run the producers gave everything away. They'd bought this cheaply and painted it purple. I had it covered with a mustard-coloured velvet. I've still got it. It's been everywhere with me.'

1960

1 January	Voiceover for TV at Film House
11 January	Costume fitting at Berman's
14–21 January	Film *Foxhole In Cairo*
26 January	Meet Cecil Landeau for lunch at The Empress
27 January	Voiceover for ABC at 1 p.m.
29 January	Film *Foxhole In Cairo* (three scenes)
1 February	Film *Foxhole In Cairo* (two scenes)
4 February	Film television at Teddington
18 February	Ampex (Record) *Guardian Angel* with Ian Bannen
22 February	Record voice *Doctor In Love* at Pinewood
25 February	Voiceover at Star Sounds Studios at 11.30 a.m.
20 March	Rehearse fashion show for Michel Goma
21 March	Compere a fashion show for Michel Goma in The Cumberland Hotel (Mayfair)
29 March	Appear on radio game show *Does The Team Think?*
30 March	Appear on *Wednesday Magazine*, probably with Ned Sherrin at BBC Lime Grove Studio G
12 April	Voiceover *Hotpoint* at Olympic Sound Studios
15 and 18 April	Rehearse songs or sketches at Sulgrave Boys Club at 324 Goldhawk Road
19 April	Perform and tape at *Bull and Bush* (Shepherd's Bush pub)
1 May	Perform at *The Green Room Rag* (annual event)
21 May	Rehearsal for Battersea Gala
26 May and 1 June	Sitting for the painter John Norton
7–8 June	Rehearse a new number for *Pieces of Eight* at the Apollo
10 June	See Sammy Davis Jnr at the Pigalle Cabaret Club, Piccadilly
12 June	Radio broadcast from BBC Paris Cinema
15 June	Photoshoot with Bob Dear
20 and 22 June	Sitting for John Norton

22 June	Attend Noel Gay charity lunch. 'They were a music publisher on Denmark Street.'
23 June	300th performance of *Pieces of Eight*
28 June	Sitting for John Norton
29 June	Rehearse at Weekes Studio with Jack Barnett (pianist), for forthcoming Palladium
3, 10, 17, 24, 30, 31 July	Appear in radio broadcast *Something To Shout About*
4 July	Photoshoot with Edgar Brind
6–8 July	Rehearse at the Palladium
11 and 13 July	Rehearse at the Palladium
12 July	Record at the Paris Cinema
21 July	Band call, *Night of 1,000 Stars* at the Palladium
26 July	Sitting for John Norton
7, 14 August	Appear in *Something To Shout About* (radio)
10 August	Meet Yvonne Caffin at Café Royal then shop for costume jewellery for *No Love For Johnny* film
10 August	Final sitting for John Norton
13 and 15 August	Fitting at Raymond Ray for *No Love For Johnny*
16–17 August	Film *No Love For Johnny*
23 and 31 August	Record *Something To Shout About*
8 September	Voiceover *Pascals Pastilles*
11 and 17 September	Appear in *Something To Shout About*
18 September	'Oh, I think this [entry] means that I dumped Mike and started dating Robin Midgley.'
30 September	Attend Tea Party at Saville Theatre for Theatrical Ladies Guild
10 October	Appear on magazine show *Home Grown* on Southern TV
16 October	Record an early audio version of *So Much To Remember* for Michael Barclay
26 October	Camera rehearsal in Studio 5B for *Reprise* (TV play)
27 October	Camera rehearsal at 10 a.m. for *Reprise* and then Ampex (record) 5–6 p.m.
29 October	Last performance of *Pieces of Eight*
1 November	See *Foxhole In Cairo* in Chelsea Cinema. 'I got a derisory round of applause from the audience when I threw the dagger into Gloria Mestre's back at the end ('Cow', with an exclamation mark and a drawing!)'
7 November	Post-sync voice for *No Love For Johnny* at Pinewood
7 November	Photoshoot with Terence Donovan at 4 Yeomans Row at 3 p.m.
11 November	Sitting for Nicholas Egon (painter) 'I went two or three times, but it drove me potty as I couldn't spare the time, so he finished it without me.'
15 November	Rehearse and record *So Much To Remember* (for Michael Barclay)
15 November	See *Beyond The Fringe* (Cooke, Moore et al) at The Establishment

29 November	Meet Michael Barclay re. *So Much To Remember*. 'We heard the recording and decided it didn't work as a voice-only piece.'
4 December	Broadcast *Something To Shout About*
5 December	Voiceover *Flair* (magazine)
7 December	Lunch with Billy Wallace at Mirabelle's in Curzon Street. 'I was photographed on my way out.'
16 December	Lunch with photographer John Cowan
18 December	Broadcast *Something To Shout About*
29 December	Fitting with Joan Ellacott at Berman's for a revue

1961

5 January	Photoshoot with Terence Donovan
7–8 January	Appear in radio broadcast *Something To Shout About*
9 January	Photoshoot with Terence Donovan
10 January	Film *Carry On Regardless*
11 January	Film at Pinewood (presumably *Carry On Regardless*)
12 January	Voiceover *Rolex*
15 January	Appear in two radio broadcasts, *Something To Shout About*
5 February	Rehearse radio play *Auguste*
7 February	See *The Importance of Being Oscar* 'A marvellous one man show by Micheál Mac Liammóir. I went with Tony, whoever he was.'
10 February	Record *Auguste*
11 February	Transmission of *Auguste*
12, 19 and 26 February	Appear in *Something To Shout About*
5, 12 and 19 March	Appear in *Something To Shout About*
16 March	Appear on *Tonight* TV show with Ned Sherrin from Lime Grove
17 March	Attend press show for *Carry On Regardless*
24 March	Go to Leicester to do publicity for *No Love For Johnny*
28 March	Go to Birmingham to do publicity for *Carry On Regardless*
2, 9, 16 and 23 April	Appear in *Something To Shout About*
20 April	Fitting for stage show *As You Like It*
23 April	Appear in *Something To Shout About*
1 May	First night of *As You Like It* (Pembroke Theatre in the Round)
14 May	Appear in *Something To Shout About*
28 May	Appear in TV broadcast of *Does The Team Think?* quiz show (Lime Grove)

29 May	Rehearse at Bromley for forthcoming double bill (directed by Vladek Sheybal)
6 June	Appear in a double bill: Tennessee Williams' *Hello From Bertha* and Prosper Mérimée's *To Heaven In A Golden Coach*
15 June	Last night of *To Heaven In A Golden Coach*
16 June	Vidal Sassoon at 11 a.m. and then photoshoot with Terence Donovan at 3 p.m. for *Town* magazine
19 June	Voiceover *Wood Pigeon* at Film House, Wardour Street
19 June	Went to Grosvenor Gallery with Bob Gill, 'that well-known shit.' (A boyfriend at the time.)
21 June	Voiceover *The Millionaires*
26 June	Fitting with Raymond Ray
28 June	3 p.m. Vidal Sassoon
30 June	Film at Pinewood, *In The Doghouse* 'My almost-cousin, Mont, saw it and said, "I expect you needed the money".'
1 July	Fitting with Raymond Ray
1 July	See *Oliver* on stage. 'Ron Moody was in the cast.'
3-5 July	Fittings with Raymond Ray
7 July	Photoshoot with Philip Gotlop
19 July	Photoshoot with Vivienne at 4 p.m.
20 July	Rehearse songs with Carl Davis at Weeke's Studio at 4 p.m. (probably for Edinburgh Festival)
21 July	Film *In The Doghouse* (scene 11) 9 a.m. Pinewood
22 July	Rehearse songs with Carl Davis at Weeke's Studio at 4 p.m.
22 July	See the show *Stop The World I Want to Get Off* (Starred Tony Newley)
24 July	Film *In The Doghouse* at Pinewood
31 July–4 August	Start rehearsals for a revue *Five Plus One* at RADA to be performed at Edinburgh Lyceum. 'The producers were Oscar Lowenstein and Michael Codron. They were both very mean!'
27 August	Fly to Edinburgh
28 August	First night of *Five Plus One* at Edinburgh Lyceum for one week
3 September	Fly home from Edinburgh
6 September	Voiceover *TV Times*
24 September	Appear in *Something To Shout About* (Series 3)
1, 8, 15 and 22 October	Appear in *Something To Shout About*
11 October	Voiceover *Scotties Tissues*
18 October	Sitting for the painter John Norton
26 October	Begin rehearsals for *The Rivals*
12 November	Appear in *Something To Shout About*

12 November	Rehearse *The Rivals* at home. 'I injured my eye. Went straight to Moorfields.'
14 November	First night of *The Rivals* (It ran for four weeks)
19 November	Appear in *Something To Shout About*
3 and 16 December	Appear in *Something To Shout About*
4 December	Voiceover *In The Doghouse* recorded at Soho Square
9 December	Last night party for *The Rivals* in the theatre bar
12 December	Attended party held by the photographer Terry Donovan and his wife Janet
20 December	Voiceover ATV Television at 6 Hanover Street

1962

(various) January	Rehearse *Twists*, originally performed in 1961 at Edinburgh Fringe as *Diversions for Five*
21 and 28 January	Appear in radio broadcast *Something To Shout About*
5 February	First night of *Twists* revue in Coventry
15 February	Fittings for *Twists*
15 February	Interview by BBC for *In Town Today* at Arts Theatre
16 February	First night of *Twists* at Arts Theatre, London
27 February	Compere dress show at Woolland's in Knightsbridge
10 March	Last night of *Twists* at Arts Theatre
12–14 March	Rehearse *The Dog Next Door* 'We all played dogs. I was a Labrador.'
19–21 March	Rehearse then broadcast radio play *Dog Next Door*
19–12 April	Record *The Rivals* for radio broadcast
17 April	Record radio play *The Liar*
20-21 April	Photoshoot with David Bailey for *Vogue* (location was Portobello Market)
25 April	Appear on *Woman's Hour*. 'They all wore hats in the studio! It was weird. I felt they were looking down on me because they were wearing hats and I wasn't.'
26 April	Appear on TV show *Tonight*, directed by Ned Sherrin. 'I did a topical song and dance number. It was a try-out for Ned.'
27 April	Voiceover at Hammer House
27 April	See Lenny Bruce perform at The Establishment
30 April	Rehearse *The Whip* (an old melodrama) 'I was the villainess. I'm certain I got run over on the railway tracks. I appeared in lots of riding clothes. I don't think I came on horseback, but I remember Jane Wenham did, lucky girl.'
1 May	Photocall for *The Whip* at Madame Tussauds
11 May	Attend party for *Old Dark House*

12–13 May	Rehearse *The Whip* at Granada
23 May	Begin filming *Old Dark House*
26 May	Retake on some photos with David Bailey for *Vogue*
26 May	Lunchtime interview for *The Sunday Times* supplement at the Caprice
2 June	Dub somebody else's voice at Shepperton for *The Main Attraction*, possibly for Nancy Kwan
15 June	Complete filming *Old Dark House*
19 June	11 a.m. met Basil Dearden at Pinewood 'Don't know what for.'
19 June	Vidal Sassoon 12.45 p.m.
19 June	Attend Al Kaplan's party went with Bob Gill
22 June	Filming at home by Granada TV
25 June	Rehearsals at the Oval, Brixton Road
25–26 June	Wig fitting
26–27 June	Rehearse *That Was The Week That Was*
28–30 June	Run-throughs for *That Was The Week That Was* at Lime Grove Studios
2–4 July	Rehearse *Stories from Saki* in Manchester for a TV series
5 July	Record *Stories from Saki*
5 July	Take the sleeper train from Manchester back to London
6 July	Vidal Sassoon at 11.30 a.m. then photographed for *McCall's Magazine*
7–9 July	Rehearse *Stories from Saki* in London
12 July	Record *Stories from Saki* in Manchester
19 and 26 July	Record *Stories from Saki* in London for a TV series (various rehearsals beforehand)
2 August	Record *Stories from Saki* in London (various rehearsals beforehand)
4 August	Appear on Harry Worth TV show (comedy) from Blackpool
9 August	Record *Stories from Saki* in London
14 August	Meet Michael Codron (producer) and Donald McWhinnie (director) re. Muriel Spark's play *Doctors of Philosophy* 'Lots of good stuff in the script.'
29 August	Rehearse *Rhyme or Reason* (TV poetry programme)
1 September	Record *Rhyme or Reason* for TV broadcast
3 September	Rehearse Muriel Spark's play *Doctors of Philosophy*
15 September	Appear on *Juke Box Jury* (TV music show)
2 October	First night of *Doctors of Philosophy* at Arts Theatre
4–5 October	Rehearse *The Double Gallant* for BBC Radio, Grafton Studios Tottenham Court Road
8 October	Record *The Double Gallant* for broadcast on BBC Radio
9 October	Attended Variety Club lunch at Savoy Hotel at 1 p.m.
4 November	Last night of *Doctors of Philosophy* at Arts Theatre
20 December	Rehearse with Dave Lee at Lime Grove Studios

21 December	Fitting at TV Centre
22 December	Appear in the try-out of a brand-new TV show *That Was The Week That Was* (from Lime Grove Studios). I did the Herbert Farjeon number that goes, 'I've danced with a man who's danced with a girl who's danced with The Prince of Wales'.
30 December	Sitting for artist Felix Topoloski. 'This was at his studio near Waterloo Station. He did a pencil drawing.' (Note: it's now a bar called Topolski)

1963

3 January	Appear on BBC TV *In Town Today*
6 January	Appear in *Monitor*, a BBC arts programme
22 January	Appear on *Day By Day* for Southern TV, recorded at TV Centre Southampton. 'I sang a song.'
29 January	Photocall for the play *Luv* at St James's Hall
4 February	Camera rehearsal at 11.30 a.m. Recording at 8 p.m. for *Mr Duncannon*
11 February	Appeared on *Does The Team Think?* – a BBC quiz game
18 February	Appeared in a radio play (in verse), *Proteus*, with Tony Britton
27 February	Voiceover *Cadbury's*
28 February	Appeared on Bernard Braden's TV show *Braden Beat*. 'It was rather posh to be invited on it.'
7–8 March	Rehearsed *That Was The Week That Was* at BBC Lime Grove Studios
9 March	Live performance on *That Was The Week That Was*
18 March	Start rehearsing *Luv* (Written by Murray Schisgal, Dick Emery appeared in it.)
17 April	Appear on *Wednesday Magazine* at BBC TV Centre
24 April	First night of *Luv*
29 April	Film *Doctor In Distress* at Pinewood
6, 7 and 13 May	Film *Doctor In Distress* at Pinewood
19 May	Last night of *Luv*
28 May	Photoshoot for *Radio Times* magazine at 2.30 p.m.
29 May	Attend Midsummer Banquet at Mansion House (A clip of Fenella arriving at this was used in *Hotel Deluxe*, a recent BBC4 documentary she narrated.)
17 June	Meet with Billy Chapel (a revue director)
20 June	Appear on Radio 4 *Woman's Hour*, possibly in a section called *Dear Abi*
23 June	Rehearse poetry with Patrick Garland for Stratford-upon-Avon programme
27 June	Photoshoot with Norman Parkinson for *Queen* magazine
30 June	Perform in poetry programme at Stratford-upon-Avon

1 July	Begin rehearsals for *So Much To Remember* at The Establishment. (A play Fenella wrote with her friend Johnny Whyte.)
2 July	Photoshoot with Lewis Morley for *Daily Mail* (to accompany interview) 'This was in Louis Morley's studio above The Establishment in Greek Street. He took those famous photos of Christine Keeler there.'
11 July	Rehearse *Night of 100 Stars*
12 July	Appear on *Seen at 6:30* on Granada TV
22 July	First night of *So Much To Remember* at The Establishment.
17 August	Last night of *So Much To Remember* at The Establishment
20 and 29 August	Photoshoot with Peter Laurie for *Vogue*
2 September	Rehearse *So Much To Remember* for transfer to Vaudeville Theatre in West End
4 September	Photoshoot with Peter Laurie for *Vogue*
9 September	'I had a day off!'
17 September	First night of *So Much To Remember* at Vaudeville Theatre
29 September	Appear on *Kitchen Party* with Fanny Craddock at Lime Grove Studios
7 October	Photoshoot with Alec Murray for *Town* magazine
9 October	Voiceover *Gillette*
25 October	Appear on *Braden Beat* (TV)
2 November	Last night of *So Much To Remember* at Vaudeville Theatre
4 November	Rehearse Comedy Playhouse *Comrades In Arms* for TV
11 November	Record Comedy Playhouse *Comrades In Arms* for TV
13 November	Interview for *Woman of Beauty* magazine
2 and 5 December	Photoshoot with Roy Round. 'I was wearing dungarees. A sort of plumber look!'
13–14 December	Rehearse *Who Is Secombe?* at Shepherd's Bush Theatre
15 December	Record *Who Is Secombe?* a 'TV Movie' at Shepherd's Bush Theatre
28 December	See *The Muffled Report* at The Establishment
29 December	See Fellini film *8 ½*

1964

11 January	See the Beatles at Astoria, Finsbury Park, 6.40 p.m. 'I took Ken Tynan's little girl, Tracie. At the end I took her backstage to meet the band. She melted when I introduced her to Paul McCartney.'
13 January	Lunch at Mirabelle's in Curzon Street with Pete Rogers and Gerry Thomas. 'I turned down the lead role in *Carry On Cleo*.'
27 January	See Maria Callas in *Tosca* at Covent Garden Opera House

29 January	Fly to New York on holiday. 'I'd say "it was to see things", but actually it was to be with a boy, which went very disappointingly; at one point quite frightening. He was on the phone to somebody while we were having a difficult conversation. Each time he turned to the phone his face lit up and each time his face turned to me it was fury. It was the most frightening thing I've ever seen. It was like he went potty each time his smile went; his face went from red to white and back continuously as he was carrying on the conversation with a lady friend and then turning to me. I should have stayed in London and done *Carry On Cleo*.'
14 February	Fly home
15 February	Rehearse *Avengers* episode *The Charmers*
26 February	Record *Avengers* fight scene
27 February	Record *Avengers* episode
28 February	Voiceover *Corgi* (toy cars)
11 March	See Stan Getz at Ronnie Scott's
23 March	Begin rehearsals for *Divorce Divorce* with Patrick Macnee, an episode in *Love Story* (series of TV plays)
7 April	'Ampex' [A type of tape, so this means 'record'] *Divorce Divorce*
10 April	Voiceover and photoshoot for *Vitalis*, a men's hair tonic. Photos show Fenella 'approving' and 'disapproving' of men who do or don't use the product.
13 April	Attend *Playboy* party. 'Fantastically chic – the Americans gave very high-grade parties at posh places.'
6 May	Begin rehearsals for *Ides of March* (a radio play in verse)
29 May	*Ides of March* broadcast
3 June	Appear on *Celebrity Game* TV show from Wembley Studios
6 June	Appear on *Gazette* ABC TV in Manchester
26 June	TV recording of *So Much To Remember*
28 June	Appear in *Line Up* (magazine programme) on BBC2 from TV Centre
29 June	Fly to New York. 'I don't know whether this was love or work.'
3 July	Fly home
15 July	Photoshoot with Terence Donovan to advertise '*The Observer*'
17 July	Terence Donovan retakes for *The Observer* ad
23 July	*Night of 100 Stars* midnight matinée
31 July	Videotape recording of *Importance of Being Earnest*. 'Also in the cast were Patrick Macnee, Ian Carmichael, Susanna York, Irene Handl and Pamela Brown.'
4–5 August	Go to *The Observer* car at 8 a.m. – possibly an interview
4 August	Dinner with Doris Lessing at 7.30 p.m.
6 August	Photoshoot with Angus McBean (a well-known front of house theatre photographer)
9 August	Poetry reading in Stratford-upon-Avon

10 August	Holiday in Athens, which was payment for recording the *Get Fit* ski flexi disc
7 September	Start rehearsing musical of stage production *High Spirits*. There are rehearsal photos of Fenella flying around the stage on wires, but she didn't appear in finished production. She was sacked by a 'terribly nice' man representing the American producers who wanted the American actress who had appeared in the show on Broadway. 'The whole thing was hateful. The scriptwriter was terrifying. It was rare that somebody be so horrid.'
19 October	Voiceover *Tio Pepe* (sherry)
22 October	Photoshoot *Belvedere Cigarettes* at Woburn Abbey
29 October	Oxford Union debate – annual humorous debate using one celebrity per team. 'Probably James Robertson Justice on the other team.'
6 November	Rehearse *Animal Land* for Yorkshire TV
9 November	Record *Animal Land* in Norwich
13 November	Appear in *Stars and Garters* music hall show broadcast for TV
16 November	Record *That's For Me* for radio with Ronnie Cass, Stanley Myers, Peter Myers (not related) and Johnny Whyte
18 November	Appointment at Vidal Sassoon
20 November	Appointment at Vidal Sassoon. Typically these appointments are weekly but extra ones are also slotted in before appearances. It might have been for a set or a comb-out to 'keep the fringe looking straight and blunt'. The stylist was often Ricky.
22 November	Appeared on *The Eamonn Andrews Show* on TV
1 and 8 December	Appeared in *Stars and Garters*, music hall on TV
9 December	Photoshoot with Terence Donovan
16 December	TV ad *Peter Stuyvesant* cigarettes. Directed by Klaus Peter Adam – a film director.
18 December	Photoshoot with Jeff Bernard for *Town* magazine
26 December	Appear on *Juke Box Jury*
31 December	Appointment at Vidal Sassoon. 'This was the night Vidal's was absolutely crammed, girls on the stairs – sitting on the floor waiting; all waiting to get their hair done. Some cried because they would be so late for a New Year's Eve party.'

1965

1 January	Interview for *Woman and Beauty*. The editor asked Fenella to pluck her eyebrows while doing an interview for a piece on beauty tips. 'So I did. I plucked the eyebrows for the editor of *Woman and Beauty* and she was jolly pleased.'
5 January	Lunch at the Caprice with a journalist called Christopher Kininmonth

8 January	Christopher Miles was a producer and he wanted to make *Fenella Fielding's Edgware* (Rather tongue-in-cheek in response to recent *Shelagh Delaney's Salford* programme on TV. 'I think we wrote a great deal of stuff and amused ourselves brilliantly but didn't actually do it.')
12 January	Appear on *7 o'clock*, Radio Caroline at Rodmarton Mews
21 January	Appear on *Woman's Hour* with Anne Howells
22 January	Photoshoot for hats designed by 'Clive the Milliner' at 17 George Street. 'He was quite important at that time. If Clive liked the way you dressed, that was good.'
23 January	Appear on *Pete Murray Show* (radio)
26 January	Appear on Radio Caroline
28 January	Vidal Sassoon in the morning
29 January	Appear on *Does The Team Think?* for BBC Radio, recorded at Paris Cinema
29 January	Dinner with Brian Clemens (screenwriter and TV producer)
1 February	Photoshoot for *TV Times*
3 February	Meet Michael Baldwin at Jaeger Café. 'He was the costume designer for the *Izeena* TV series.'
5 February	Rehearse *Izeena* in London
7 February	*Izeena* rehearsal in Norwich
8 February	Record *Izeena* for Anglia TV
10 February	Interview with Anne Hooper for *Photoplay*
12 February	Voiceover *Paws* cat food
16 February	Take part in Cambridge Student Union debate that *This Union Should be Consummated*
17 February	Interview for ITN *Dateline*. Recorded 10.15 p.m., aired 11 p.m. 'This was to raise money for the Roundhouse Theatre (Camden).'
1 March	Judge a beauty contest at the Lyceum
4 March	Photoshoot with Peter Deal for *Harper's* feature *Beauty Fruit*
10 March	Meet Fay Weldon who had just written a play – a comedy about going on a diet. 'It was never made. I did some stuff of hers later.'
18 March	Take part in London University debate *This House Advocates Polygamy*
19 March	Meet Brian Clemens. 'It was to discuss doing a TV thing. I can't remember what, but it never happened.'
22 March	Appear in anti-apartheid *Midnight Matinée* at Prince of Wales Theatre
24 March	Voiceover *Littlewoods Pools*
25 March	Meet actress Hermione Gingold who wants to perform *So Much To Remember* written by Johnny Whyte and Fenella. 'Fortunately it never happened. I'd have hated anybody else to do it.'
29 March	Photoshoot for *TV Times*. 'What was wrong with the first lot I did in February? That's what I'd like to know.'
1 April	Read-through of *Mrs Quilley's Murder Shoes* at ATV

3 April	Late-night radio appearance on *Pete Murray Show*
9 April	Voiceover for chocolate. 'Not sure which ones.'
10 April	Photoshoot for *Woman* magazine
20 April	Record *Mrs Quilley's Murder Shoes* for ATV
22 April	Voiceover *Carson's Liqueur Chocolates*
25 April	Rehearse with Ronnie Cass
1 May	Voiceover *Macleans Toothpaste*
6 May	Meet Derek Monk at ATV House (Probably about *Mrs Quilley's Murder Shoes*)
10 May	MGM record scene 33. 'Probably a studio test for something that didn't work out.'
11 May	Record *Sing a Song of Sixpence* at Wembley Studios 2 p.m.
14 May	Appear at the Dorchester for *The Television Society*
15 May	Rehearse for *Memoirs of a Chaise Longue* (Comedy Playhouse)
18 May	Voiceover for *Ellida*
21 May	Record *Memoirs of a Chaise Longue* (Comedy Playhouse) at TV Centre
24 May	Meet Arnold Wesker, a well-known writer for The Royal Court and a member of Centre 42 (an association of political writers). 'This was about fundraising for a new pillar for The Roundhouse.'
31 May	Attend playback of *Memoirs of Chaise Longue*
2 June	Photoshoot for Carzell's *Woman's Mirror* (section in *Daily Mirror*)
3 June	Rehearse with Ian McPherson (pianist)
4 June	Record music with a pianist 'Barry Cawthery' at Associated Rediffusion Studios
8 June	Voiceover *Dwight Wear* clothing
16 June	Photoshoot with Anthony Blake. 'I was wearing hats.'
18 June	Appear on *Woman's Hour* on BBC Radio
22 June	Bandcall for *You're On Your Own*. 'I sang a song on TV'
23 June	Record my horoscope cast by *Celeste*. 'She was a horoscope woman. It was released as a flexi disc given with *Nova* magazine.'
26 June	Record *Izeena* in Norwich (flew there from Stansted)
2 July	Voiceover *Gale's Honey* at Dean Street, Presby Studios. 'As a result, I had about ten tons of honey to take home!'
7 July	Voiceover *Remington*
8 July	Voiceover for furniture
12–14 July	Rehearse *Man and Superman* for radio (Bernard Shaw play)
14 July	Record *Man and Superman*
28 July	Read through *Izeena* at Brook House
29–30 July	Rehearse for *Izeena*
8 and 16 August	Record *Izeena* in Norwich

4 August	Photoshoot for *Woman's Mirror*
5 and 13 August	Rehearse *Izeena*
8 and 16 August	Record *Izeena* in Norwich
8 August	Record *Alice In Wonderland* for an LP. (Fenella played the Dormouse. Bruce Forsyth and Karen Dotrice were also at this session.)
16 August	Listen to *Man and Superman* broadcast
18 August	New wig for *Izeena* from Wig Creations
30 August	Appear in *Points of View* at BBC TV Centre
31 August	Meet Jean Hamilton for first time at Claridge's. 'She took over as director of *Izeena* because it had become a bit camp. It was her who wanted me to change the wig and have longer hair. It looked much better.'
3 September	Photoshoot with Peter Laurie
4 September	Appear on *Pete Murray Show* (radio)
7–8 September	Rehearse *Izeena*
9–10 September	Record *Izeena*
12 September	See Shirley Bassey at Pigalle (cabaret club). 'She was very good!'
13–14 September	Rehearse *Izeena*
15–16 September	Record *Izeena*
23–24 September	Rehearse *Doctor In Clover*
27 September	Whole day of fittings at Wig Creations, Berman's and Raymond Ray (dress maker, he did the dress for *Old Dark House*). 'This was all for *Doctor In Clover*.'
28–29 September	Film *Doctor In Clover*
30 September	More fittings for *Doctor In Clover*
1 October	Film *Doctor In Clover*
1 October	Meet with John Hart at Baron's Court to learn dance for *Giselle* scene in *Doctor In Clover*
2 October	Fitting with Raymond Ray for *Doctor In Clover*
4 October	Film *Giselle* scene for *Doctor In Clover*
4 October	Dinner with John Mortimer at Pickwick Club, Newport Street
11–15 October	Film commercial for BP
18 October	Interview for *Woman's Journal*
20-21 October	Riding lessons for Tony Curtis film *Drop Dead Darling*
28 October	Voiceover for Rank Overseas commercial
29 October	Perform in *Man Speaking* radio show
1 November	Lunch at Shepperton, then fitted with wigs for *Drop Dead Darling*
2 November	Photoshoot with John Cowan
3 November	Fitting for wedding dress (3 p.m. at West Street) for *Drop Dead Darling*
3 November	Appear on *Juke Box Jury* 7 p.m. till 9 p.m.
4 November	Stills photoshoot at Shepperton Studios

10 November	Pre-filming medical with Dr Hadge at St Georges Hospital. 'I was still having riding lessons in Hyde Park!'
14 November	Dinner with Ken Hughes (director of *Drop Dead Darling*)
19 November	Filming for *Drop Dead Darling* begins. It continues till 8 December. 'There were a few days I wasn't called.'
28 November	Appear on *Call My Bluff* on BBC TV at Television Centre
8 December	Stills photoshoot for *Drop Dead Darling*
12 December	Take part in poetry reading at Stratford East with Robert Stephens (National Theatre actor). 'It put me onto a completely different part of my career.'
17 December	Visit 12 Connaught Place for the first time. 'I moved in shortly after.' (Moving from Hyde Park Square.)
20-21 December	Photoshoot with Peter Deal
23 December	Insurance check-up with doctor for a film
23 December	Record voiceover for *Doctor In Clover*
31 December	Record with Mike Sammes Singers. 'It was pros. Something to do with England playing France, possibly in the World Cup.'
31 December	Paris House to choose costume jewellery for *Carry On Screaming*, 3 p.m. 'I bought the ruby ring myself. It was £9, which was a lot to pay then for a piece of rubbish.'

1966

3 January	Wig fitting for *Carry On Screaming*
6 January	Record *Newsreel* on Nile Street
7 January	Voiceover *Shell Mex*
12 January	Film *Carry On Screaming* at Pinewood
13 January	Post-sync voice drop, *Drop Dead Darling* – Shepperton car at 8.15 a.m.
17 January	Filmed scenes 89 and 90 of *Carry On Screaming*. Rehearsals and filming for continued till 7 February 1966 (except Saturdays & Sundays)
22 January	Moved to Flat 4, 12 Connaught Place (Marble Arch) 'I paid £13 a week for five rooms, which was the entire top floor!'
18 and 22 February	*Carry On Screaming* (Pinewood), possibly voice work, starting at 7 a.m.
25 February	*Carry On Screaming* stills photoshoot at 8.30 a.m.
28 February	Fitting for *Doctor In Clover* 11 a.m.
3 March	Fitting *Doctor In Clover*
3 March	Appear on *Roundabout* at noon – a news/entertainment TV programme, with Keith Harrison
5 March	Interview with Shirley Lowe for a magazine
7–9 March	Film BP commercial at Shepperton, probably directed by 'Haliford'
10 March	See rushes of *Carry On Screaming* at 58 Wardour Street

11 March	Ideal Home Exhibition. 'I went in a Rank Car so it must have been a promo for them.'
14 March	Interview with Carl Conway for Radio Caroline
28 March	Photoshoot for *Doctor In Clover* at Odeon, Edgware Road
31 March	Voiceover for film *My Last Duchess* Post-sync a poem by R. Browning and fill-in work.
4 April	Record TV commercial for BP *Big Visual* at Delaine Lee Studios
12 April	Meeting at Shell Mex (South Bank)
28-29 April	Personal Appearances for BP
2 May	Start rehearsals at Mermaid for *Let's Get a Divorce*
6 May	Personal Appearance for BP
11 May	Wig fitting
11 May	Molly Kenny prepare movement for *Let's Get a Divorce*
12 May	Voiceover at 20th Century Fox, Soho Square
22 May	Interview with Roger Snowden at Broadcasting House 8.30–9.30 p.m.
29 May–1 June	Dress rehearsal for *Let's Get a Divorce*
2 June	First night of *Let's Get a Divorce*
5 June	Appear on *The Eamonn Andrews Show* on BBC TV
6 June	Interview with Herbert Kretzmer, showbiz journalist
8 June	Interview with Hunter Davies for *Sunday Times*
9 June	Bush House for BBC appearance
10–11 June	Company call/rehearsal *Let's Get a Divorce*
12 June	Travel from London Airport to Troon for BP personal appearance
13 June	Photoshoot at BP Autocare Station. (Fly from Glasgow to London at 2.40 p.m.)
13 June	Meet Eric Thompson at Golden Egg (café) in Marble Arch
20 June	See Billy Graham preaching, probably at Wembley – 'Fascinating'
6 July	Rehearsals begin for *Let's Get a Divorce*, which is about to transfer to West End. 'We were getting used to a different stage – the Comedy Theatre.'
19 July	Photocall for *Let's Get a Divorce*
23 July	Finish run of *Let's Get a Divorce* at the Mermaid
26 July	First night of *Let's Get a Divorce* at Comedy Theatre
27 July	Travel to Cambridge for BP personal appearance
2 August	Travel from Euston to Oldham for BP personal appearance
5 August	Meet Laurie Johnson about a musical, *Four Musketeers*. 'I don't think I did it, but I remember going on an aeroplane with Laurie. He was terrified of flying and had to take a tablet to knock himself out.'
8 August	Fitting for *Let's Get a Divorce*. 'It was an upgrade to my costume.'
11 August	Trade show for *Carry On Screaming* Studio 1 (a cinema in Oxford Circus)
11 August	Interview with Bill Hall (columnist) for *The Evening News*

14 August	Appear on *Call My Bluff*, hosted by Frank Muir
15 August	Press luncheon at Warner Theatre for *Carry On Screaming*
18 August	Personal appearance in Leeds for BP
19 August	Personal appearance in Brighton for BP
28 August	Meet James Roose Evans (Then the director at Hampstead Theatre. He later made the film *84 Charing Cross Road*.)
31 August	Appointment at Nathan's (a costumier)
1 September	Personal appearance at Datchet Green for BP
6 September	Appointment at Nathan's 11 a.m. then Wig Creations at 3 p.m.
12 September	Photoshoot with Peter Lawrie
16 September	Appointment at Wig Creations 10.30 a.m.
22 September	Q&A at the English Speaking Union London School of Economics, 12.45 p.m.
25 September	Appear on *Call My Bluff*, hosted Frank Muir
29 September	Photoshoot with 'WM' (?) for BP
30 September	Personal appearance in Sale, Cheshire for BP
2 October	Appear on *Call My Bluff*, hosted Frank Muir
7 October	Retake photo still with 'WM' for BP
11 October	Interview with Carl Conway for Radio Caroline
12 October	Perform *The Rivals* on the radio
13 and 16 October	Work with Carl Davis and George Mully to prepare the song 'Big Bad Mouse'
17 October	Record 'Big Bad Mouse' at Stage Sound, 2–5.30 p.m. (It was released as a single on Columbia Records.)
18–22 October	Rehearse *Hedda Gabler* for BBC Radio in studio B10
23 October	Record *Hedda Gabler* for BBC Radio
23 October	Meet Patrick Macnee
25 October	Personal appearance in Pulborough for BP
30 October	Lunch in Sydenham for BP
1 November	Listen to first edit of *Hedda Gabler* at Broadcasting House
21 November	Interview with Ed Stewart for Capital Radio
22 November	Sitting for the painter Vasco Lazzolo at EMI 3 p.m. 'It's for an exhibition – probably for BP.'
24 November	Sitting for Vasco Lazzolo at EMI 2.30 p.m.
25 November	Interview for *Woman's Own* magazine
28 November	'We're still doing '*Let's Get a Divorce,* although Barry Foster is off.'
5 December	Interview with Colin Hamilton for BBC World Service
6 December	'Gerry Sharp, a friend, helped me buy some new hi-fi from Imhof's on Tottenham Court Road.'
13 December	Attend Variety Club Christmas Lunch

15 December	Sitting for Vasco Lazzolo
16 December	Interview with John Peter for *The Times*
17 December	Rehearse with Carl Davis for recording on 19 December. 'He was hugely fussy about every single note.'
18 December	Rehearse with Carl Davis
19 December	Record 'Professor' and 'Big Bad Mouse' at CBS (Not sure why the latter was recorded as it had already been released as a single b/w 'Later'.)
20 December	Rehearse with Denis Cooper the songs 'A Day, A Year, A Lifetime', 'It Didn't Work Out' and 'Everyone Was Very Understanding'
21 December	Record voice at MGM Studio for *The Prisoner*

1967

Note: *Let's Get a Divorce* is still running from 1966 and continues till 22 April this year

1 January	Appear on *The Eamonn Andrews Show*
5 January	Interview with Paul Callan for *Evening Standard*
10 and 11 January	Voiceover *Cadbury's*
18 January	Press show of *Drop Dead Darling*
24 January	Record spoken part for *Road to Saint Tropez* for Mike Sarne at 20th Century Fox, Soho Square
3 February	Sitting for Martin Wright (sculptor), who is working on a head
6 February	Appear on *Call My Bluff*
7 February	Give poetry reading at London University Senate House
14 February	Dorchester Hotel for a gathering in advance of a Chichester theatre performance
16 February	Sitting for Martin Wright (sculptor)
2 March	Voiceover to replace somebody in 'Wicked Lady' (possibly a film) at 60 Greek Street
6 March	Attend event in 'Top of the Tower' restaurant (Post Office Tower) for National Society of Mentally Handicapped Children
March-April	'Mr Scarr appears a lot here. They're often two-hour appointments – it was probably driving lessons. I didn't ever take the test. I was much too nervous.'
20 and 21 March	Rehearse at Broadcasting House
23 March	12–2 p.m. Broadcast from studio L1, Broadcasting House
27 March	Meet Fellini at Claridge's Restaurant at 1.15 p.m.
12 April	Voiceover *Newsreel*
18 April	Voiceover *Newsreel* and dubbing *Breck Hairspray*

20 April	Voiceover *Bel Air Hairspray*
22 April	Last night of *Let's Get a Divorce* at the Comedy Theatre
24 April	Rehearsals for *The Beaux' Stratagem* (in Chichester) begin in London
30 April	Sitting for Martin Wright (sculptor)
1 May	Appear on Radio 4's *Desert Island Discs*
7 May	Rehearse for *The Beaux' Stratagem*
5 June	First night of *The Beaux' Stratagem* at Chichester
26 June	Start rehearsing *Italian Straw Hat* (to follow on at Chichester) Note: it was to have been *Servant of Two Masters* with Danny Kaye, but he pulled out so the play was changed.
2 August	Last night of *The Beaux' Stratagem* at Chichester
6–7 August	Dress rehearsals *Italian Straw Hat*
8 August	First night *Italian Straw Hat* at Chichester
27–28 August	Rehearse *Pygmalion* for radio
29 August	Record *Pygmalion* for radio
16 September	Gala night in Chichester – 'I did a turn'
17–19 September	Went to Enton Hall. 'It was a health farm!'
25 September	Rehearsals begin for *The High Bid*. Directed by Bernard Miles, co-starring Edward Woodward.
15 October	Technical run-through *The High Bid*
16 October	Dress rehearsal *The High Bid*
18 October	First night of *The High Bid* at The Mermaid
20 October	Interview with Angus McGill for *Evening Standard*
23 October	Interview with Desmond Lyons for *Daily Mirror*
25 October	Interview with Patricia Johnson for *Evening News*
18 November	Last night *The High Bid*
27 November	Appear on Kenneth Robinson radio show
30 November	Interview with John Peter for *Sunday Times*
6 December	Appear on *Magic Box,* a TV show recorded in Teddington
20 December	Appear on *Choice of Paperbacks* (radio show) with two distinguished writers
21 December	Reception to meet the Smothers Brothers (an American comedy singing duo who provoked controversy with their material critical of the political mainstream).

1968

3 January	*Tennis Elbow Foot Game*, radio game show broadcast from Paris Cinema
9 January	Luncheon at Lord Mayor's Mansion House
(various) January	*Tennis Elbow Foot Game* radio game show broadcast from Paris Cinema
23 January	Sitting for Martin Wright (bust)
28 January	Appear on *Call My Bluff*
2 February	Meet Robert Erskine (boyfriend) for lunch at Cranks, Marshall Street. (Fenella often arranged to meet people there. It was one of the few vegetarian restaurants in London at the time.)
7 February	Voiceover at De Lane Lea (Sound Studio)
13 February	Interview with John Peter for *Sunday Times*
19 February	Voiceover *Pedigree Dolls* at Advision, New Bond Street
21 and 28 February	Appear *Tennis Elbow Foot Game* radio game show
25 February	Poetry reading at Chichester
6, 13 and 20 March	Appear *Tennis Elbow Foot Game* radio game show
27 March	Fitting for *Lock Up Your Daughters* (film) at Berman's (West Street)
5 April	Meet Hal Burton (translator/director) re. solo play for the BBC – *A Touch of Venus* (part of a series of plays). 'It was very posh to do a play for Hal Burton.'
11 April	Fitting at Berman's for *A Touch of Venus*
15–17 April	Rehearse *A Touch of Venus*
18 April	Fitting at BBC TV Centre
20 April	Record *A Touch of Venus* (solo play) at BBC TV Centre
21–22 April	Filming *Lock Up Your Daughters* begins in Kilkenny
26 April	Interview with Catherine Stott (columnist)
30 April	Meet John Peter at Gay Hussar (restaurant in Greek Street)
1 May	Interview with Catherine Stott
4 May	Filming *Lock Up Your Daughters* continues in Kilkenny (scene 27) then home
12 and 15 May	Filming *Lock Up Your Daughters* continues in Kilkenny
17–18 May	Filming *Lock Up Your Daughters* continues in Dublin
27 May	Rehearsals for *Dear Lady* – part of new a TV Series *Ooh La La* (Feydeau Farces)
12 June	Voiceover for North West at De Lane Lea
13 June	Rehearse *Call Me Maestro* (Feydeau Farces) for TV
15 June	Record *Call Me Maestro*
1 July	Rehearse *Missing Person* (Feydeau Farces)
4 July	Fitting for *Missing Person*

6 July	Record *Missing Person*
15 July	Rehearse *Two Whole Days* (Feydeau Farces)
5 August	Rehearse and record *Does The Team Think?* for radio at Paris Cinema
16 September	Rehearsals for *Lysistrata*, a Greek comedy, begin at Oklahoma University ahead of Fenella's arrival
21 September	Fly to New York then Oklahoma (a place called Norman)
23 September	Rehearse *Lysistrata*
24 and 26 September	TV promos for *Lysistrata* in Lawton, Oklahoma and Tulsa
1 October	Press conference for *Lysistrata*
2-20 October	Full rehearsals begin for *Lysistrata* (Greek comedy)
21 October	First night of *Lysistrata* at Oklahoma University Theatre in Norman
26 October	Last night *Lysistrata*
31 October	Fly home via New York
4–8 November	Rehearsals for *The Seeker* begin in Nottingham
24 November	Dress rehearsal for *The Seeker*
26 November	Preview of *The Seeker* in Nottingham
27 November	First night of *The Seeker* (repertoire so not continuous, but runs till 31 January 1969)

LIST OF ILLUSTRATIONS

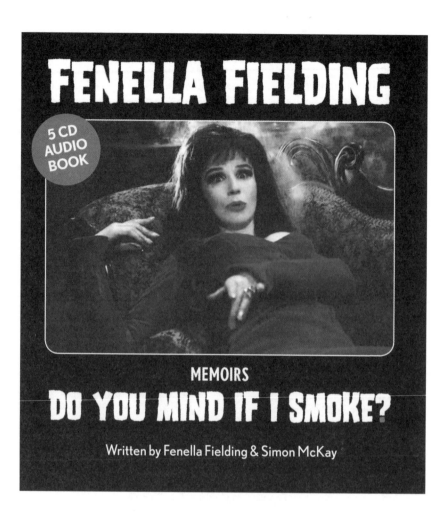